Advance Praise

"If you are facing a challenge in your business, Tara Pickford has been there and has found a way forward. *Teaching Ambition* is the place where she shares those lessons and experiences. Whether you are starting new or starting over, now is the time to focus on growing your business!"

—Misty Lown, Founder and CEO More Than Just Great Dancing!®, Misty's Dance Unlimited, YPAD, Chance to Dance Foundation

"Tara Pickford brings a wealth of knowledge and business acumen in this information-packed book about successfully owning a business in the cultural sector. *Teaching Ambition* is a must-have guide for anyone at the beginning of owning a performing arts studio and a call to action for established businesses to discover best practices. Her anecdotal experiences and lessons offer invaluable information on goals, finances and planning, all while pursuing your dream of being a successful entrepreneur. Her colloquial style injects humour and levity that make this a wonderful read. She gets you excited about your vision and dreams and offers you so many critical tools to do so. She creates so many actionable items for businesses to put in place immediately, and that will affect their long-term success and profitability. Customer service, staffing, e-commerce, finances, marketing, and so much more, *Teaching Ambition* is a bible for anyone who runs a tuition-based business!"

—Jay T Schramek, Owner of Toronto Dance Teacher Expo, Dance Attack Competitions, and Tap Shoes Canada

"*Teaching Ambition* will open a door for younger dance teachers and studio owners who can learn and apply many of the suggested steps to better business management and operational skill development in a tuition-based business. Tara Pickford is open and honest regarding her own personal journey and, more importantly, proving that success must be earned. She encourages the acceptance of bad decision-making as a learning tool. Accepting small failures is part of building a successful business. All dance studio owners should read this book. *Teaching Ambition* has much to offer for any business owner or entrepreneur who is hungry for more financial success."

—Brian Foley, renowned dance teacher,
director and choreographer

"If you are a dance studio owner or thinking about opening a studio, run and get this book! Tara Pickford's experience and life journey as a studio owner, teacher, and resilient leader is the perfect "HOW TO" to do this right! From the initial details of start-up and buildout, all the way through the challenging and creative ways she pivoted her businesses, *Teaching Ambition* is a complete blueprint to master the success of owning a dance studio or any business successfully."

—Tracey Wozny, Entrepreneur, Youth Educator,
Non- Profit Founder, Speaker, Shapes Dance
and Acro Studio and Taking Shape

"I recommend *Teaching Ambition* to anyone who wants to work for themselves but is hesitant to take the leap due to fear of failure. This book really gives the reader a gentle push into following their dreams and desires, but most importantly, it gives you all the tools you will need to make it happen."

—Kelly Konno, Owner of Kelly Konno Studios

"*Teaching Ambition* touches on everything from vision and mission to leases and buildouts. It's really a one-stop-shop for a micro business owner. I would share this with salon owners, restaurant owners, boutique owners, and any other small-scale entrepreneur."

—Melanie Gibbs, Founder of Pro Am Dance Studios,
Boca Dance Studio

"Starting a new business, struggling in your current business? Tara Pickford gives amazing insights and action items you can implement immediately! Her life and business experience are excellent examples to help you find shortcuts in your own entrepreneurial journey."

—Kevin Bender, Phoenix, AZ. Small Business
Owner and Entrepreneur

TEACHING AMBITION

Growing Your
Tuition-Based Business

TARA
PICKFORD

Pickford Consulting Ltd.
210 Cooperstown Lane SW
Airdrie, AB T4B 2L2
Taralpickford@gmail.com

Tara Pickford, author
Tami Hutchinson, cover art

ISBN 978-1-7778291-2-4   Paperback
ISBN 978-1-7778291-3-1   eBook

First Edition

This book is dedicated to my "WHY." I have moved heaven and earth for you both, Tia and Trissa. I love you more than you will ever know.

Table of contents

CHAPTER 1 – OVERVIEW

Whether you think you can or think you can't, you are right.

Henry Ford

Are you doing today what you thought you would be when you were growing up? How about when you decided you were going to open a business? Is the day-to-day what you imagined? Yeah, my life does not look anything like what I thought it would be!

Today I am a serial entrepreneur. I did not set out to be this way. I never saw this lifestyle coming. It was not even what I thought I would be growing up, not even close. I am sure those around me would say the same. Here I am today, owner of several companies, an international speaker and author, a mom, a partner and most importantly, a fulfilled person who knows her "why" and what success looks like to me. I am the most peaceful I have ever been.

It wasn't always that way. My journey was definitely the long way—no shortcuts and some double-backs. Hard-learned lessons, huge failures and small victories. I won't even hazard to say that I am anywhere close to done learning, growing, or creating. I bet you are not either, or you would not be reading this book!

This book is full of my biggest burnouts and great successes, but most of all the many lessons in life and business I learned along the way to get where I am today. It is my honour to share my growth and hopefully some wisdom gained along the way, so you too can start, learn, and lead.

And it begins...

My mom enrolled me in dance lessons when I was three. As most parents do when they see their child take an interest, they try to develop that interest. For me, it was dance. I was a highly scheduled kid. In the '80s, there was no such thing as special classrooms for those of us who learned faster, processed quicker, or needed more challenges. Most teachers gave extra writing assignments as a reward for work completed well before the rest of the class—not much of a reward if you ask me.

My mother recognized that I needed more and did her best inside of the family budget to keep me as active and challenged as possible while growing up. Between dance, figure skating, soccer, softball, Girl Guides, organ lessons, school sports teams, school plays, band and clubs, I learned to manage my time and still stay at the top of the class fairly effortlessly. I had no problem skating early mornings, going to school, dancing after school—all while maintaining my homework load and my friendships. As I grew up, I began to enjoy the challenge of: "How much can I fit in before my schedule just can't expand to take it all in?"

All this to say, I have always been an overachiever. It's where my sweet spot is. However, one of the afflictions of an overachiever is that you never feel like you have accomplished anything. It's why I keep driving hard; I just want to achieve something that feels satisfying.

As high school came to an end, it came time to make some tough decisions about my future. After many contentious conversations with my dad, I begrudgingly agreed that I would obtain a university degree before pursuing a dance career. This was pivotal because many dance careers don't last beyond age 25 or 26 for commercial dancers, and I believed I was spending my most employable years as a dancer at university instead. I completed high school with honours and went on to achieve my Bachelors of Kinesiology, Major in Mind Science, Minor in Dance.

Upon graduating, I received a scholarship to go to Los Angeles. At home, in preparation for going to LA, I worked hard and saved as much money as I could. I made plans to move in with some friends who were already there and start the life that was put on hold while four years of university happened. I bought my plane ticket, quit my three jobs, broke up with my boyfriend, packed my bags, and eagerly awaited the next amazing stage of my life. Then, a BOMB. The friend I was moving in with called the night before I was to fly out. The studio doors had been chained up that morning – "out of business" was the rumour. My scholarship was dead in the water.

DEVASTATION... I waited four years to have this happen – longer than four years. More like 10 years when I decided I wanted, no, *needed* a career in dance. What was left? Just teaching and working as a personal trainer and kinesiologist? How drab. I never wanted any of this as a career.

TEARS... I wanted this SOOOOO BAAAADDDD. I had been working incredibly hard. I played by the rules. I got the degree, then pursued the rest. This is unjust!

ANGER... University was a bad choice. It sucked the best performing years of my life. One of my life's regrets was that I caught my dad's glance that night. In the terror of my life falling to pieces, he was smiling smugly. He hadn't wanted that life for me. The look still follows me in my mind. I know now it was his relief showing in a strange smile. I know he only wanted a life of abundance and happiness for me. He came from an era where he couldn't see how this could be a good choice for someone as smart and equipped as I am. But in that moment, it was daggers to my heart.

FEAR... What now? I had no job, no direction, no boyfriend, and now what? I had never been unscheduled before. I had been highly overachieving my whole life. Where do you start finding direction when there is none?

Dry your tears, throw your hair in a bun, put on some gangsta rap, and handle it. I went on the best two-week vacation with the money I had been saving. I flew to LA anyway. I took classes, many classes, with master teachers I admired. I crashed auditions with no agent (thrilling!). I went to Soul Train. We drove to Vegas with a hotel coupon from a bank machine receipt we got 20 minutes earlier. We ate cookie dough in the hot tub and dreamed our wildest dreams out loud. Cheap wine, terrible amounts of cheap wine, the stuff where bad decisions loom at the bottom of the bottle. We had the time of our lives in beautiful, crazy, exciting and dangerous, sunny LA. Then I packed my suitcase and came home. I asked for two of my jobs back – no need to work three anymore – and I asked my boyfriend if he was free that night. He was. And life marched on.

I put the education my dad was adamant about to good use and worked as a personal trainer and weight room floor manager during the day and taught dance at night, putting in 70-hour weeks as my regular week. As a high achiever, schedules like this give me fuel in the tank. I did this for nine years, minus my two-week LA stint.

I married a boy. He worked at the company I was a trainer at. Here's how it started: One of my dance moms hired me to create a bodybuilding routine for her. I would meet her at her gym and put the routine together for her. I was fresh out of university, desperately trying not to be a trainer. I was still trying to get to LA. She had a list of required poses and I would link them together. There was a trainer who was creeping past the fitness studio window every few minutes.

The mom I was training said: "I think he is trying to get a better look at you," and winked. I said: "That's insanity, too cliché to get picked up in a gym." Well, I got picked up in a gym, but not until after I got hauled into the manager's office to explain why I was training someone in their gym without permission or paying fees. Once we got it cleared up that I was not "training" anyone, but I was in fact choreographing, a service they did not offer, their client found me. The trainer who had been creating all the grief for me asked me to dinner. I said yes. His manager asked me to apply to work there. I did that too.

I began working as a personal trainer on April 1st, April Fool's Day. That whole irony has never really escaped me. The career I had desperately tried to avoid because it is an easy trap for a kinesiology degree and I fell into it, April 1st, 1999.

It wasn't all bad. I learned to run an outdoor pool program, group fitness classes, hire, and fire. I eventually became the weight room manager. But it wasn't something I loved. I loved to teach dance. I tolerated my fitness career. Eventually, that trainer became my boyfriend, and the boyfriend became my fiancé, and then my husband. It all happened fast in the span of just over a year! He loved this life. He loved his career. He still does and he is amazing at it. It just wasn't for me. Eventually the company experienced some wonderful growth that had a need for higher-level positions and we both had our name in the hat. One of us would be the other's boss. It was already a challenge to work for the same company, and as a female in a male-dominated industry that in itself took its toll, this ask was too big. I did not love this career, but he did, and he should take all the opportunities he could. I stepped away from the company and he stepped up into the role.

I took a job managing contracts for renters in our local community hall. It was a pit stop while I was still teaching. Just a paycheque and some experience on contracts and facility management – all experience that would come in handy if I ever pulled the trigger to do something more. I also went back to the gym and started selling memberships, gaining sales experience that also would come in handy soon.

Then I broke my foot... It was really bad.

I was subbing a maternity leave in the fall of 2002 at another studio (where I grew up), and that fateful night set everything into motion. I broke my foot and shredded the tendons and ligaments. It was a pretty catastrophic injury because of how it happened. I was demonstrating a jump that changed direction in midair and jumped higher than my landing anticipated. It was like a movie: everything slowed down, and all the students were in a circle crowded above me with their heads shimmering in the light from the room as I looked up.

The break was pretty bad: six weeks, non-weight-bearing, giant air cast, and dismal hopes for returning to the range of motion I had enjoyed up to 24 hours previously. I felt confident in my teaching skills that even without being able to show the steps, my classes would not suffer, that I could just as easily use my words. A good teacher should be able to use many ways to reach the class. This would be a chance to grow myself in another way as a teacher. Challenge accepted. My boss at the time and I had a bizarre conversation that I still remember word for word to this day. She did not see the positive in this at all.

"I have hired an assistant teacher for you. She will be paid a portion of your hourly wages," my boss announced.

"That was not necessary," I replied. "I didn't ask for help, and there are several students who would take that role as a volunteer just for the chance to learn to teach." I had it all planned and figured out already.

My boss wasn't having any of it. "It is already decided, and they have been promised pay. So you will be working for reduced wages until you are able to demonstrate again."

"Is it in my contract that I have to demonstrate?" I asked

"No," she replied.

"Do I still need to create the lesson plans?" I pushed, knowing the answer.

"Yes."

"Do I still need to be on time?"

"Yes."

"Am I still the adult in charge when I am there?"

"Am I still responsible for the student outcomes?"

"Am I responsible for the assistant being trained to help?"

"Am I still opening and closing the facility?"

Yes, yes, and yes, the answers came back.

"Can you please explain how all of this leads to less pay for me?"

"I don't have to. It has been decided." My boss ended the conversation there.

At that moment, my world snapped around in the blink of an eye. As long as I worked for someone else and my job was physically demanding, an injury could prove to be devastating in many ways. Not only was I dealing with a potentially permanent injury, but I would also have to do the same amount of work for half the pay and train someone who was taking my wages at someone else's whim. What strange dimension had I entered? If I had been in charge at that moment, there is no question that the employee would not be docked. Or I would at least give the employee the chance to show they shouldn't be docked, or maybe have a conversation around assistants that we could both agree on.

It was the last straw in a list of many ways that I felt this position was no longer for me. At this point, I felt I had paid my dues. I had a lot of ideas on how I would do things, and I had learned what I wouldn't do while working for others. I felt stifled in my position because there was no way to implement what I felt I really needed to do as a teacher to get the results I knew the students were capable of. I had gotten into trouble a few times, been written up while I tried to stretch in my role. It became clear that I needed to create my own space to be able to do what I was really capable of.

It was a heart-wrenching choice. The woman I worked for was a brilliant ballet teacher. I admired her deeply. She had been my teacher for many years until I began to work for her. I had given her school seven years of my teaching career. I really became a great teacher because of the challenges her business model provided me. But this was the start of a terrible tension between us that made our last season together unbearable, and that tension sadly still exists today. Dance is passionate, and when you mix business and passion, there is much room for heartache. I wish she could see how much she did for me. Even in the difficulty, the tear-filled nights of feeling wronged no matter how much right I tried to do by her, she taught me the level of professionalism I would need for the next step of owning a business. She toughened my skin, and Lord knows the path I was headed on was going to need more than tough skin.

When I decided to open my own business, I knew I could create something special. With my training, knowledge, and teaching experience, I felt I had something special to give that was unique.

Action Item

Grab your favourite journal and find a quiet place. Take some time to be focused and introspective when you answer these questions. Dive deep into this. The answers are so important to help you moving forward. It is really important to know where you've been and take stock of how your life has shaped you into who you are today. Here are some questions to get answers to:

- What did you want to be when you grew up?
- How did it evolve or change over the years?
- What major life events have you been through?
- How did they shape or change your views?
- Where are you now?
- What do you want to be remembered for?
- "The Dash" Year born to the (dash)Year died: what do you want to accomplish during your dash? What will your impact be?
- What do you want people to say about you when you are gone?
- How can you start living today for the way you wish to be remembered?

CHAPTER 2 – STARTUPS AND BUILD-OUTS

> *The beginning of wisdom is to call things by their proper name.*
>
> *Confucius*

A Name to Stand Out

I spent hours planning how my school would be different from the places where I had been working. How it would be dance taught scientifically. How we would be a full-fledged performing arts school, training triple-threat students (singing, dancing, and acting). We would change the industry standards. We would be the place where everyone would want to train. We would get results like no other school. I dreamed hard about every aspect.

I read all the business books I could get my hands on at the library, tried to get all the advice. I toiled over a business name and the best way to go about it.

Important Note:

Below are some tips on selecting a name. If you go through these and start to think that you may need to change the name of an existing business, that can be done too!

- *Something that starts with "A" will be listed first in many directories.*
- *Don't put your own name in the title so that the exit plan is easier.*

- *It has to describe your business.*
- *It needs to make clear what you are selling.*
- *It should be something that can be made into a web URL (at the time I made mine, short and sweet was the key — not the case today).*
- *Can it be an acronym?*
- *And what else is that acronym used for?*
- *Can you trademark it?*
- *Is it different enough from the rest of the market?*
- *Should you register it provincially, federally, or internationally?*

So many things to consider. It was a huge decision. Once the name was decided, I was off to the registry to do the name search and start making a company from my ideas.

Incorporation vs Proprietorship

A big business starts small.

Richard Branson

I researched whether I should spend the money to incorporate or wait to see how it all unfolded. I decided to incorporate because of the nature of the type of business. It seemed smart to protect our family assets from potential liability lawsuits in the future.

I made the decision to save money and register the company myself. I had no idea what I was doing and bought a "do-it-yourself kit" and set up my own books for $200. That was a decision that would later become a large bill with a lawyer to fix the things I did wrong. I did not know you needed to record annual minutes into your minute book and how to keep it updated or why you would want to. I was the only person registered on the books for the company. It said "president," but I was also vice president, treasurer, secretary, and janitor!

Some things are not worth the sweat equity. You really have to know your limitations and make use of what you can do and what would take little time to learn. Hire an expert for the things you really struggle to wrap your head around. It is good to have an understanding, but you cannot be the expert at all things. Know your sweet spot.

Finances

I knew to keep track of the expenses during start-up and I used a spreadsheet in the beginning. Finance was never a strong suit for me until recently when I set a personal goal to get a strong handle on it. I knew that you should never just hand your books over, but I had no skill set for this. What did I know about cash flow, projections, budgets, proformas, and saving for a rainy day?

How do you create a budget when you have no idea what the expenses are going to be? And by the time you know what the expenses are, you are so overwhelmed with all the other operations of the business that you never circle back.

We ran our first six months without books set up at all, keeping track of receipts in a folder and on bank statements. When we started to have too many transactions, we hired a parent at the studio who had a bookkeeping background. The problem was that I didn't know what to pay her and what skills I needed to actually hire for. It turned out she was not as qualified for the job as we needed her to be. Then we had the uncomfortable problem of releasing a paying client who thought she was doing us a favour but being paid for the favour and doing a poor job. It was difficult and messy, but we had to move on so that we could get to the next level.

I decided to go to the local college and took accounting courses specific to software. I took both level one and level two courses in Simply Accounting. That is when I realized that I couldn't do everything and I was not passionate about bookkeeping. I hated those few months. Instead, I should have been finding a better expert and interviewing bookkeepers. I don't regret the education because it gave me the knowledge to find my way around much better in Simply Accounting and then in QuickBooks when we made the switch. The education from this course serves me every day as I go into the program and move around in the financial statements. I can find my profit-and-loss statements, I can navigate a balance sheet, and I can understand the entries and why they're booked the way they are. I can find the data I need to make everyday business decisions, budgets and proformas with five-year projections. This knowledge allows me to keep track of what's happening, even though I have hired it out to another expert. Any knowledge that helps you understand what is happening is good, but I had too much other work to do to be the bookkeeper as well. I highly recommend learning what you need to know to navigate the program and then hand it off to an expert who is proficient.

Hire people who play at what is work to you. Talk to other business owners and ask them who they use, what they like, what they don't like. Use this information to build your interview process for vendors. I did change accountants and bookkeepers a few times as my business grew, my needs changed, and my knowledge flourished. This is a part of growth. Do not stay with a vendor too long. Healthy things grow and change. You need vendors who can grow with you too.

It became evident that we were patching things together with the wrong people and not enough knowledge when, after three years in business, the opportunity to grow a second location presented itself and our books were a hot mess. They had been set up wrong; thousands of wrong transactions and a few thousand dollars to fix and bring up to date so that we could explore the growth opportunity. The problem with bad books is that the opportunity can pass you by. They take a long time to get fixed and provide the reports you really need. But you are also operating with bad data. How can you steer a company if you have no idea where your money is going and what it is doing for you?

Important Note:

Lesson 1: *Get help with the things that are your weakness. The couple thousand I saved at the start became a huge bill three years later that was more than double what it would have cost to get the good advice from the beginning.*

Lesson 2: *I hired a bookkeeper – that is not the same as an accountant. I also took several bookkeeping courses at a local college because you are always told to never give your books to someone else and to not understand what was happening inside them.*

Never give your chequebook to someone else. I still, to this day, write all the cheques. We now have a new database, where the office can do refunds but only to previous purchases, and they do not pay out expenses.

I hired an accountant. It is really important to find an accountant that understands your business and can help you plan, save, and make smart choices. I have switched accountants seven times in 18 years. I just could not find that person who could help me the way I believed accountants should. Currently, I have finally found the right one. Someone who will look across all my businesses and see the cycles they go through and how to plan and prepare for each one. I literally went across the country to find her. Not all accountants are the same, and they are not made equal. Not all businesses are the same and you need to be sure you find the right expert for your company. If you are hiring out to an expert, make sure it is the right expert.

Mentors and Coaches

A coach is someone who can give correction without causing resentment.

John Wooden

I didn't realize it at the time, but I was using two of my uncles as mentors. They helped me with advice and questions as they came up. One was especially helpful in educating me about leases and agreements with owners. The other uncle provided business acumen and reason when I would get so emotionally attached to the outcome that I would stop thinking clearly. He had taught me early on that no matter how much you wanted that job, the contract wording was important, and to never sign something that you don't understand or may not be able to live with if the worst case happens.

I read so many books at the beginning that I did not seek out a business coach until I was further along in my journey. In my city, there is now a program offered to new businesses where they can be partnered with a local business owner who volunteers to be a mentor and help them get their business going in the first year. I am happy to now be a mentor in this program. I would have been happy to have something like this. I felt terribly isolated and scared to make such large decisions on a daily basis during those first few years. A mentor would have been everything to me.

Important Note:

Look for local programs where business owners who are in the giving stage are willing to mentor new owners. Look for someone you admire, take them to coffee or lunch, and use the time to gain precious bits of knowledge. Check with your local Chamber of Commerce and business organizations for startup programs.

Leases

Location, location, location.

Lord Harold Samuel

If you are opening a brick-and-mortar business, think hard about where your clientele lives and how they will access you. People want services in their neighbourhood. In large cities, people might drive 20 minutes, but likely closer to 10-15 minutes to get to you. Who is your target? For us, it was young moms. We needed to be in new neighbourhoods where there were going to be lots of babies born in the next 10 years to feed our programs. The problem with this is that space in those neighbourhoods is at a premium. Yes, you might find cheap warehouse space in the industrial park, but those new mommas are not driving their precious babies to the industrial park for classes. They want to grab a Starbucks and pedicure while their child learns how to do ballet or another class in a safe community that matches their values.

Leases are tricky. They are worse if you have an owner who is a large company and doesn't trust you to fulfill your end of the bargain. We can forgive their reluctance when you are a startup with no books/financials to show proof that you can pay them. It is imperative that you have a lawyer to ensure that you have not literally signed your life and your family savings away. Also, that lawyer will help you negotiate options to renew at the end of the term. An option to renew means that you have the first right to renew the lease before the owner opens the search to the market.

A typical option to renew might look like a five-year lease and a five-year option. Meaning you lease for five years and have the option to renew for another five years. This is crucial if you are building the space out and don't want to rebuild again when the lease is up. Moving into a new space is expensive, especially if your current leaseholds still have a lot of life left in them. Returning a space to its original state when you leave a lease is also expensive.

Having to do both is a special kind of pain – paying to leave and to get a new space prepared for business. If you do not have an option to renew the lease, the owner does not have to keep you as a tenant and is free to shop your space around when your lease is up. Having an option protects your investment into your leaseholds. These are huge expenditures, especially as a startup.

Some parts of your business are enormous business deals, the kinds that make or break your profits in the future. A lease is one of those. It is important to have an experienced lawyer in this type of law who helps you understand how the clauses you agree to could come back and take shape in the future. I have seen too many people sign bad leases, and they go under paying the owner obscene sums of money. These deals happen because they did not know the lawyer was out of scope, or they decided they couldn't afford the right counsel at a critical time.

My first location had a five-year lease with a five-year option, meaning it had a lease for five years where we could opt to stay an additional five years. We exercised the option and were there for 10 years. However, when I exercised the option, we did not negotiate a new option and with six months left on the lease, I contacted the owner to discuss the renewal. They wouldn't even return my call. I was kicked out even though I wanted to stay. I had to walk away from all the money invested in the space (dance floors, barres, mirrors, flooring, walls, lighting fixtures, bathrooms, built-in desks, shelving, etc.). It had been well maintained and would have lasted at least another 10-15 years with a fresh coat of paint. These were all tenant improvements that I had paid for. Walking away from it all was like watching my money and time be set on fire. How many lessons had I sold to pay for it all? I can tell you at $50 per month and a $200,000 build-out, I had to teach 4000 lessons. That was 4000 hours of my time, not including the sweat equity I had put in at the beginning to keep costs down. Expensive lesson learned. We had to walk away from all of it, knowing someone else would likely demolish it to create a space that suited their needs for their new lease. And they did. The new tenant gutted the space.

Buildout

Sweat equity is the most valuable equity there is. Know your business and industry better than anyone else in the world. Love what you do or don't do it.

Mark Cuban

Once I signed a lease, it was time to find a contractor to help with the things our sweat equity could not do alone. Where do you start if you have never used a contractor before? My dad was a genuinely clever handyman. If he didn't know how to do it, he taught himself. Commercial is different. You need to use a ticketed journeyman to get inspections past the city and for your insurance to be valid. I did some asking around, and eventually we found three quotes from people that I did not have strong ties to. We managed to narrow it down to the one who was willing to work with us the most, allowing us to use our sweat equity to bring down the buildout costs.

Today I have created community relationships where I could get a much better referred contractor. Knowing what I know now, I would interview the heck out of the people who referred the contractor. I would try to get a hold of people who used him and weren't on his referral list. The contractor we chose did great on the first job; we hired him again when we opened our second location. But he took the money and never paid the trades and overpriced the job substantially. Always vet the contractors, even if you believe you have a previous relationship that is strong. You never know what is happening in their company that would make them turn bad, but they can, and they do.

Realize that you do not have to have all the bells and whistles to get the door open. Make a list of the things that are nice to have but don't stop the doors from being open. Give yourself financial goals that allow you to cash flow the last parts of the buildout, allowing more freedom and less debt to get off the ground with.

25

In a dance studio, that means: the barres and mirrors are nice but not a deal-breaker if they come a few months down the road. For a clothing store, it might mean some displays are purchased later. For a quick, casual restaurant, maybe the fancy menu boards are later and cardstock menus are how you start.

Database

Data beats emotions.

Sean Rad

We opened huge. At the time, I was too naive to know what I had done. Ignorance is bliss, right? Everything I had done: all the research, the painstaking lease agreement, the buildout with my own hands to save money, creating classes, schedules, marketing, hiring the first few teachers and office staff had all been amazing. And now the students were pouring in.

That's when the big lessons began...

Most people don't realize that to really be a business you can't just get yourself a job in the company. You need to be able to work on the company, not just in the company. If you just want a job, stay working for someone else. If you want a legacy and an impact, build a business.

Most business books are written for small businesses – 50 to 250 employees. The majority of family businesses are actually micro-businesses with 20 employees or fewer. This is impactful information because we are still trying to compete against companies that have 30+ more employees than we do. We need the same marketing strategies, social media, 24/7 customer care – but with way fewer resources.

I had no database other than a spreadsheet with 230 students. This quickly became a nightmare. Managing classes, payments, and account changes was awful and not my strong suit. We ran for four months before I realized I had no idea what I was doing. It was a huge mess. I mentioned above that I took an accounting course to ease this pain and burden, but what I really discovered is that I cannot do it all, nor am I expected to. I am expected to steer the ship, and I needed to make decisions fast about how our course would be corrected.

I researched databases for how to manage my students, the classes they were in, and the billing and payments. I didn't know what else I needed the program to do, as we were in our first year. I encourage you to look beyond the immediate problems and try to project the growth or needs your company could face given the direction you are planning to take it. At the time, I didn't realize that buying a program to use as our database was actually expressly forward-thinking. Most owners were using spreadsheets at that time. The problem I saw was that we opened huge, I had big plans to grow, and spreadsheets were not efficient. I wanted to teach amazing classes, not lose my mind in data entry. I had worked in fitness clubs. I knew there was another tech out there. I just had to find it.

You don't know what you don't know until you know it. This is why mentors and relationships with other owners in networking groups are important to your success. They can help you find resources you didn't know about and envision needs you will have before you realize it.

Action Item – Type of Business Structure

Do the research and think hard about what type of business is the best type for you and the industry you are in. There are three main types:

1. *Sole Proprietorship – owned and operated by a single individual*
2. *Partnership – owned and operated by two or more people*
3. *Private Corporation – a legal entity registered with government, assets and liabilities are separated from owners*

Action Item – Finances

When you are looking to hire experts for your business, and you're trying to decide how much a service or expert is worth to your budget, use this rule:

- *How much is your time worth per hour?*
- *How much time will this task take you?*
- *How much is an expert in the field worth per hour?*
- *How fast can they do the same job?*
- *Is their work going to be higher quality/more accurate than the work that you did?*

Once you answer all of these questions, you'll be able to determine how much an expert is worth to you and your business. Here is an example of this:

- *You earn $100 an hour because that is how much your time and expertise are worth.*
- *You are still cleaning your own home for three hours a week.*
- *You can hire a cleaning expert for $25 per hour.*
- *That expert frees up three hours a week of your time.*

It's easy math to see that hiring a cleaning expert is a better financial decision for your time and for your business. The bonus is that you get someone who's efficient and perhaps can do the job in less than three hours – creating further savings.

Important Note – Leases

Who is your customer? We want to believe it is everyone. That would mean we have lots of potential clients just waiting to find us. But it is not everyone, and not all customers are equal. Build an avatar for the variety of customers you want to attract. Then consider where they naturally hang out. Then look at how your physical location will serve them. Most businesses will have multiple avatars. Each product or service you offer is attractive to a different type of parent. For us, the parent of a program for three-year-olds is immensely different from a five-year-old's parent's needs, and again when the child is eight and so on. As a child grows, so too does their family and their needs that a program can fulfill. The avatar of a returning customer is also different from one who has yet to experience your programs or services.

CHAPTER 3 – VISION

Vision without action is merely a dream.
Action without vision just passes the time.
Vision with action can change the world.

Joel A. Barker

When we start to envision what our new company will be, we have lofty goals and huge ambitions. As the quote above states, "Vision without action is merely a dream." We need to get clear on where we want to go, so we can map how to get there, step by step. Without a clear mission and vision process to arrive at succinct end points, we struggle to gain traction.

When I started my company, all the books told me to get a mission and vision statement. Sometimes these instructions have you arrive at paragraphs. That is how I started out. I had a big wordy paragraph that I created long before I had my first customer. Having gone through several versions of these statements and having now been in business long enough to know more, my original mission statement was about me and what I wanted, not about what we were actually doing. And it definitely was not something my staff could remember, let alone execute daily.

So let's explore the first iteration of a mission statement, the first iteration of a vision statement, and how the "why" we start our business with is something that changes over time and over the experiences of who we do business with. These are statements that need to be revisited every 5-10 years to ensure they match the opportunities still available in the market and the services or products still being provided.

Whether you are alone with the task or whether you have a team to work with, this section contains activities that you will be required to do some work on.

Get clear on your vision for the future. As an entrepreneur, endless distractions will compete for your attention. Also, endless directions to take with your business can lead you off course and away from your destination. You need to be able to trust your gut and be super clear with what your vision and priorities are.

Mission Statements

Without a mission statement, you may get to the top of the ladder and then realize it was leaning against the wrong building!

Dave Ramsey

I was so proud of my mission statement when I created it. As you read this chapter, you will see how it evolved and why. This is the long, wordy sentence that I thought was just perfect 20 years ago. But as we go through the content in this chapter, you will see it go through a couple of iterations to land where I am today.

I used to hand out prizes at staff meetings to the person who knew the mission statement by heart. I thought this would get people to understand it and think about it. I was wrong. Instead they just memorized it, which was not the outcome I was looking for. A mission statement needs to be something that everyone can deliver on at all times of the day inside the company. A big, long, cumbersome statement does not serve that purpose. In all honesty, I had to look it up if I wanted to use it – even I struggled to remember it word for word, and I wrote it!

Version 1:2002 to 2008 – 6 years of business:

Our Mission: *To be an industry leader and innovator through exceptional training in Performing*

> *Arts, while providing programs oriented around education, performance opportunities, health and awareness, life skills, friendships, and positive self-esteem.*

Your company needs a mission statement to help direct its reason for being. To help carve a way forward, shape decisions, and stay true to its main focus. It helps employees understand the core values, decisions made, and direction taken. It unifies all efforts toward the one thing that the company exists to accomplish.

A mission statement will help you to establish your identity, attract the right type of employees, and guide the culture inside your walls. By shaping your purpose clearly, you can set the stage for the level of performance expected, construct the behaviours needed, and ignite the critical thinking needed to achieve the mission.

Your company mission statement should describe what you are doing, right now, every day. It should discuss the benefits of how you do things. It does not say how you are doing things. Something that's really helpful to get started is creating a list of words that are important to you when describing what your company does. You may choose to use a word cloud of feedback from clients, or you might ask your staff to provide words that come to mind when they think of your company. The purpose of this is to start to see which words best describe what you are doing right now.

If you are not in business yet, start creating a list of words that are important to you to shape the message that your business provides. There are several free online word cloud generator tools that you can use to upload words to see what the most common words are that are used in your company or in reviews by customers. This will help you set the framework to get started.

A Mission Statement Should:

- Be a clear and concise declaration of your business strategy
- Provide a framework for employees for the purpose of the company
- Speak to your market
- Provide information on the product or service you offer
- Provide a distinction about you from the rest of the market
- Be achievable, encouraging and unique
- Be no more than 10 to 12 words – it is a statement, not a paragraph; choose the words well

I always look to large successful brands to see what they are doing for inspiration and example. It is no secret that these companies spend large amounts of dollars to come up with these statements. I look to them to see how I can model myself and learn from their large budgets.

Examples of Mission Statements for Large-Brand Companies:

- *Apple:* To bring the best personal computing products and support to students, educators, designers, scientists, engineers, businesspersons and consumers in over 140 countries around the world.
- *Nike:* To bring inspiration and innovation to every athlete* in the world. *If you have a body, you are an athlete.
- *Coca Cola:* To refresh the world... To inspire moments of optimism and happiness... To create value and make a difference.
- *Netflix:* To entertain the world.

- *Amazon:* To continually raise the bar of the customer experience by using the internet and technology to help consumers find, discover and buy anything, and empower businesses and content creators to maximize their success. We aim to be Earth's most customer-centric company.
- *Starbucks:* To inspire and nurture the human spirit – one person, one cup and one neighbourhood at a time.
- *Spotify:* To unlock the potential of human creativity – by giving a million creative artists the opportunity to live off their art and billions of fans the opportunity to enjoy and be inspired by it.

Vision Statements

If you are working on something exciting that you really care about, you don't have to be pushed. The vision pulls you.

Steve Jobs

For 16 years, we did not even have a vision statement. To be honest, I was not sure how the mission and the vision were different. It wasn't until Cam Hodgson of Podium Enterprises came in to speak to my staff that I started to understand the difference and why both really are needed. As mentioned above, mission is how/what we are doing today, while vision is where we will be in the future. Without a vison, you spin your wheels in the today of it all. People, including your staff, need to know that you have a vision for the future, that you know where you are going, and that you will lead them there.

Version 2: 2018 – 16 years of business:

Our Vision: We are driven to provide quality lessons in a safe, innovative and enriching environment. We hold ourselves to a higher standard while putting life skills, community, friendships and family first. Parents choose APA Dance Studio for our convenient location and friendly service, and welcoming atmosphere. They stay with us because of our commitment to excellence, value, culture and customer care.

Vision statements help companies stay on task, develop a sense of purpose, and keep employees goal setting and striving for more. It helps the company identify its organizational structure and attract talent that suits the distinctiveness of the company. This statement unites all departments under one target intention.

This should be an audacious statement about where you're going as a company and where you hope to be in the future. It is written as though you are already there. This powerful positive messaging allows you to continue to strive to be what the statement says. It is just that – a vision, which means it hasn't happened yet, but it's something that you strive to be. Be picky with your words. It should be meaningful and aspirational, and include bold statements about what you will deliver as a company. This statement should speak to how you will be the best at what you do.

It should contain clear and concise language. It should be inspiring, create a challenge to rise above, and be relevant to the identity of the business. It should take a 5-10-year forward view of what the company can accomplish. The language should say the vision is happening now, spoken as though it has been accomplished.

A well-written vision statement becomes a filter that the company can use as consideration for undertaking any new initiatives. If the initiative does not match the vision statement, then it is something that your company should not do.

A Vision Statement Should:

- Outline the organization's goals.
- Include the purpose of the organization.
- Be short, simple, and specific to the organization.
- Include some ambition – where you strive to be, be the best.
- Project 5-10 years into the future of the company.
- Describe what success looks like for the organization.
- Describe a measurable goal.

Vision Examples Here:

- *Apple:* We believe that we are on the face of the earth to make great products and that's not changing.
- *Nike:* To bring inspiration and innovation to every athlete in the world.
- *Coca Cola:* Our vision is to craft the brands and choice of drinks that people love, to refresh them in body & spirit. And done in ways that create a more sustainable business and better shared future that makes a difference in people's lives, communities and our planet.
- *Netflix:* Whatever your taste, and no matter where you live, we give you access to best-in-class TV shows, movies and documentaries. Our members control what they want to watch, when they want it, with no ads, in one simple subscription.
- *Amazon:* To continually raise the bar of the customer experience by using the internet and technology to help consumers find, discover and buy anything, and empower businesses and content creators to maximize their success.
- *Starbucks:* To treat people like family, and they will be loyal and give their all.

- ***Spotify:*** To be a cultural platform where professional creators can break free of their medium's constraints and where everyone can enjoy an immersive artistic experience that enables us to empathize with each other and to feel part of a greater whole.

For my company, we have actually had three iterations of mission statements and vision statements over the years. As more opportunities open up in our market, as we grow more into ourselves, we see the need to revisit this mission statement and update it to match the opportunities that we have taken on. Through this process, our vision statement has also changed. But what has remained the same through all of this is that each iteration of our mission and vision becomes much clearer and more succinct. Each version becomes a better filter for how we consider new undertakings and new initiatives.

The second time we built our mission and vision statements, we hired a business coach to help us as a company. This was an incredibly informative experience for both myself and my staff. I was able to see how people who have been working for me thought about our company. Seeing the words they chose also helped me realize what I needed to work on as a leader to help our company move forward toward my own goals for the company. If you have the budget available, this is an amazing experience, not only to get a very clear picture of where you are headed but also to have intense buy-in from the team. This is an investment that keeps giving to this day.

Examples of APA Mission Statements Over the Years:

Version 1: 2002 to 2008 – 6 years of business:

> ***Our Mission:*** *To be an industry leader and innovator through exceptional training in Performing Arts, while providing programs oriented around*

education, performance opportunities, health and awareness, life skills, friendships, and positive self-esteem.
*Note this one says how we will do it, and that does not need to be included.

Version 2: 2018 – 16 years of business:

Our Mission: *Our ambition is to be an innovator in dance education, developing friendships and skills for a lifetime.*
*This version has removed the how.

Our Vision: *We are driven to provide quality lessons in a safe, innovative and enriching environment. We hold ourselves to a higher standard while putting life skills, community, friendships and family first. Parents choose APA Dance Studio for our convenient location and friendly service, and welcoming atmosphere. They stay with us because of our commitment to excellence, value, culture and customer care.*

Version 3: 2020 – 18 years of business:

Our Mission: *Raising tomorrow's leaders through the arts.*

Our Vision: *Providing exemplary lessons in a safe, innovative and enriching gold standard family comes first environment.*

*We did not have vision statements until 16 years into the business.

As you can see, the longer we were in business and as we became clearer on what we were delivering and where we wanted to be, the statements evolved and became succinct, meaningful, and powerful. It becomes the thing you say when someone asks what your company does. "We are raising tomorrow's leaders through the Arts."

Power Statements and Elevator Pitches

Power is making a statement about who you are.

Christina Aguilera

The first time I attended a conference with people outside my industry was a really scary event. I was so far out of my comfort zone. I panicked about what to wear, how to interact—the best way to take notes. I re-evaluated everything I knew about conferences so I could ensure I would get the most out of them. I spoke to mentors and coaches about how to network with others who would likely think that my career was "cute" or "nice." I really wanted to show up at this event. So I learned about power statements and elevator pitches.

If you only had 30 seconds to turn the head of a really great connection that you needed to make, how would you do it? If you only had a few seconds to describe what you do and to get someone's attention, how would you do it? A power statement is the answer.

Power statements are clear messages and concise words that highlight the value and skills of you or your organization. They highlight the strength that achieves results. Think of this as your "personal pitch." If you met someone and you only had a moment to get their interest in what you do, how could you frame a statement that would cause them to ask more questions? How can you ensure that they want to ask more, that they couldn't help but ask more?

Example:

What do you do for a living?

"I own a dance studio," or "I am raising tomorrow's leaders through the arts."

Which of these answers compels you to ask more questions?

Having these statements developed and at the ready is powerful for all types of business dealings. These statements should be memorable and intriguing. These statements will help you stand out from the other conversations, applications for funding, or attendees at an event. It should add profound meaning to your career and the conversation at hand.

I can tell you firsthand that having done the work on a power statement before that conference gave me the confidence I needed to walk up to anyone in that room and hold my own. Whether they were building an empire of hospitals or a real estate firm with international offices, I belonged there right beside them.

Turning APA's Mission Statement into a Power Statement:

Mission: Our ambition is to be an innovator in dance education, developing friendships and skills for a lifetime.

Power Statement: I raise tomorrow's leaders through the arts.

The Elevator Pitch

The purpose of an elevator pitch is to describe a situation or solution so compelling that the person you're with wants to hear more even after the elevator ride is over.

Seth Godin

An elevator pitch is a thoughtful way to describe what you do. It is a succinct description of what your company does. It is a powerful tool. When crafted correctly, it compels the listener to ask more questions and engages them in an intelligent conversation. It should be persuasive and informative and last no longer than 30 seconds – the length of an elevator ride, hence the name.

This is a longer version of the power statement. This is what you would answer someone who follows your power statement with a question such as, "Oh? Can you tell me more about that?" This is where you have their attention, and you want to keep it.

When creating an elevator pitch, several things need to be considered:

- Identify your goal – what do you want the speech to accomplish
- It should explain what you do
- It should clearly state your unique features
- It should leave the listener compelled to ask questions

When you have done the above, form it all together into a rehearsed speech that you have ready for any moment it can be used.

Internal and External Pitches

Now we are diving really deep into this. As we are working on these statements, you may have started to notice that you might want to give different messages externally to new customers and vendors and an entirely different message internally to staff or customers who are already bought in. You would be right. The messages we want to send to the different groups do need to be crafted uniquely to the response that we are trying to elicit.

External Pitch (People Who Purchase Our Services):

Your external pitch provides all the compelling reasons for purchasing your services. It describes why you are the best choice for what they are buying. It confirms that there is no better choice for this purchase.

APA External Pitch

- Parents need quality programming that they can feel good about investing in.
- We provide a family-first atmosphere that puts age-appropriate development first and that teaches leadership through the arts. We do this with gold-standard business practices and technology.
- Families are able to choose their level of participation from a variety of participation commitments.
- The real magic in this lies in tailor-made schedules and experiences that foster our dance family today, as well as creating leaders for tomorrow.

Internal Pitch (For People Who Work For Us):

Your internal pitch presents all the reasons why someone should choose to work for you over other market competitors – why you are the best choice for their career goals and needs.

APA Internal Pitch

- We are the **largest studio** in our market.
- We are the only studio that offers this **variety** of programming and commitment.
- Our certified, highly **educated** team values **continuing education** and leading training tools to ensure **safe and acceptable training practices.**

- We already serve **one in 10 girls** in the Airdrie area; with our new facility in our sights, we aim to make that three of every 10 girls and to clear the **milestone of 800 students** served.

- Our goal is a **new facility** that **impacts** Airdrie Culture moving forward.

These statements, mission and vision, power and internal and external pitches, can be used endlessly. Whenever I am interviewed for the newspaper, or doing a podcast, or showing up to a new client meeting or Chamber of Commerce meeting, I am always using these. Having these statements created, rehearsed, and ready to go is super helpful. I am able to confidently deliver them and ensure that the message I want to be heard is clear and concise, easy to follow, and presents the right image for myself and my company. By using these tools that I have put so much work into, I know I will have a great meeting.

Action Item: Mission Statement

Using the words that you have compiled either in a word cloud or in a list, start to create up to five statements each of 12 words or less, using those words. It should succinctly state exactly what you are right now. If you are working with a group of staff, break them up into five groups to create their own statement per group. Give everyone a fixed amount of time to work together to come up with each group statement. Keep the timer on and the allotment short. When you come back together, have each group read their statements. As a reunited group, talk about which ones have the qualities that best match who your company is today. Using a process of elimination and the ability to mesh statements together, work toward landing on one clearly stated sentence.

Be sure to check that it does not say how you do these things, only what you are doing today.

Action Item: Vision Statement

In a similar process to your mission statement, collect several words that describe where your company will be. Then create several statements using those words. Be sure that it says "This is what we are" as though you have already arrived.

If you are working with a group of people, break them up into no more than five groups. Ask each group to create a statement using the words collected by the whole team. When everyone comes back together, present all five statements, and work to whittle them down to one succinct meaningful statement that becomes the vision of where the company is headed.

Action Item: Elevator Pitch

- Grab five index cards.
- Label the top of each:
  - Who am I?
  - What do I do?
  - How do I do it?
  - Why do I do it?
  - Why should you care?
- Create your idea list for each card.
- Create 1-2 sentences out of each card's brainstorm.
- Organize the cards/sentences into a compelling speech.
- Practice it! Make sure it is smooth and conversational – don't sound too rehearsed.

Action Item: Internal / External Pitch

The same activity from above can be repeated to build this process. Use the same tools and process, but look at it from these two lenses:

External – The clients who purchase from you.
Internal – The talent you want to hire.

Grab five index cards.
Label the top of each:
- Who am I?

- *What do I do?*
- *How do I do it?*
- *Why do I do it?*
- *Why should you care?*

Create your idea list for each card.
Create 1-2 sentences out of each card's brainstorm.
Organize the cards/sentences into a compelling speech.
Practice it! Make sure it is smooth and conversational – don't sound too rehearsed.

CHAPTER 4 – FINANCES

> *There are things we don't know we don't know.*

> *Donald Rumsfeld*

Earlier I mentioned that I went and did a *Simply Accounting* course levels one and two at a local college. I'm not recommending that this is the exact thing that someone would have to do in order to understand their finances. However, I am not sad that this is the information that I took in. Prior to this course, I had barely any financial knowledge. I understood that I needed to keep track of the money coming in, and I understood that I needed to keep track of the money I spent or paid out, but beyond that, I had incredibly little knowledge as to how finances would be able to help me grow my business.

Taking both of these courses at the level that a bookkeeper would need was overkill, for sure. However, I did gain a great amount of knowledge in how our customer accounts were recorded, how the expenses were allocated, and how I wanted to see my chart of accounts laid out to be the most meaningful to me.

Important Note:

A chart of accounts essentially means labelling all the buckets that you wish your money to go into and all your money to come out of. It needs to be cleverly laid out in a way that will help you understand what has come in and what type of sale contributes to that revenue, and what has been spent and what type of expenses create the total.

The thing about growing your business is that you will always find more meaningful ways to slice your data. Listen to that voice and work with a bookkeeper or an accountant who is willing to adjust and grow with your business and your needs for measuring and viewing your data. I have changed, adjusted, and modified my chart of account more than five times over the years. As our business grows and our offerings change and our need for more precise information grows, you need to be able to adjust the method of recording it all.

Finding the Right Professional Help

The secret of my success is that we have gone to exceptional lengths to hire the best people in the world.

Steve Jobs

What I am advocating is that you seek out the knowledge that you don't have. It is truly difficult to hire out what is not your strength if you don't understand what you were looking for. You don't have to be an expert, but you do need to know what you are looking for in a result and the basics to oversee it all. Unfortunately, this is a trap that I fell into for multiple years before figuring out how to solve it properly. I erroneously believed that every accountant would look at my books and help me understand my expenses and, more importantly, help me figure out where I was spending incorrectly. This is not the case; the majority of accountants are only trained for compliance with your local government. They are not trained to help you read your books and help you do a better job. They are not trained to look through your accounts and question agreements or contracts with vendors that might be out of line on the expense side. They are not trained to see if you are charging enough for your product or service. They are also not trained in how to help you make use of multiple corporations that you might own, which is eventually where I landed. They are only trained in compliance. Full stop. If you are relying on them for anything else, you'll be sorely disappointed, as I was, over and over again.

Ethics and Accountability

Ethics is knowing the difference between what you have a right to do and what is right to do.

Potter Stewart

I have switched accountants seven times in my 18 years owning the dance studio business, each time believing that I was switching to a professional who would help me achieve something greater than what I had already found. Each time, I was greeted with a bill that grew a little more, and a little less input on how I could make better change for my company.

I was once referred to a family member's accountant who is great at avoiding "the taxman." This for sure did not follow the ethics or morals that I govern myself with, but I had no idea how to interview a bookkeeper or accountant and the person who referred me was a successful businessman. I jumped in. That was the shortest relationship I had with an accountant, thank goodness. It wasn't until I really decided no that I was pushed into figuring out what I didn't know. I landed in a do-or-die situation. That situation was a separation that ended in divorce.

The truth is that if your business is healthy, you will pay taxes. Paying taxes is part of doing good business. Just plan for it and you will not have to play games or do crazy hijinks to "save" money from the government. Be proud that your business does well enough to be in the position to pay, and plan to pay. No worry necessary, and no games needed.

I was faced with the decision of getting a handle on everything or folding up shop. Because I'm a fighter, I decided to get a handle on it. This is what a budgeting deep dive looks like.

Pricing Your Programs and Services

It starts with looking inside each account inside your chart of accounts and peeling apart every single layer. To do it properly, you want to create a system that's repeatable and descriptive. Start with a spreadsheet where you can calculate the expenses for a program and input variables like wage, number of students, price per student, etc. It creates a bit of a sandbox to ensure you have tweaked all the variables to the best possible outcome.

Every year I attend an event called Studio Owner University®. It was at this event where I learned of the three levers you can pull to increase your revenue. Building a spreadsheet to play with these is also a great tool. The three levers you can pull are:

1. The number of customers you have
2. The amount each sale is worth
3. The number of sales per customer

		5% Increase	10% Increase	15% Increase	Change to Bottom Line
Price of Each Sale	$50	$52.50	$55.00	$57.50	@15% with 200 customers = $1500/month increase
# of Customers You Have	200 Students	210 Students	220 Students	230 Students	@15% more students = $1500/month increase
# of Sales per Customer	1 Sale	1.05 Sales	1.10 Sales	1.15 sale	@15% more sales = $1725/month increase
Turn all three dials = $4700/month increase					

With this new knowledge, I dove into every program we offered and matched the cost to our customer with our expense inside the company and realized that if it profited less than 15%, I could put my money in the money market and save myself the trouble of being in business and all the work that went with it. What I learned from this deep dive is that I had a lot of maturing to do in the accounting department. Instead of knowing my books, I feared running out of money. I was constantly moving money from one account to another, praying that I was not going to run out of money before I ran out of month.

I had to learn that it wasn't just about the money that was supposed to be in the bank at the end of the year that my balance sheet told me should be there, but it was about making sure that I had money every month to afford the business expenses as well as the home and food that my family needed. I could no longer afford to be the unpaid entrepreneur; it was time to get real, and fast. Single moms cannot miss pay cheques.

I started looking at things such as the burn rate. This is the amount of money it costs simply to have the door open, before running any programs. This is a dollar amount that includes every single expense, except for wages, for what we were selling. Rent, administrative wages, utilities, insurance, website, marketing— every single expense except for the wage of the teacher in the classroom. This allowed me to understand how many students we needed in each program to ensure that the burn rate was covered, and then we dug deeper to figure out how many more students were required to cover wages. What I discovered was alarming and disheartening. What I had been operating on was completely untrue. I believed that we needed four students to make a classroom profitable; it turns out that number is closer to 6-8 students depending on how expensive the teacher is. I had been operating for nine years with the wrong information. Just this discovery alone could have saved my business, but of course, there is always more to uncover.

When you start your business, you tend to price similar to those in the market around you. You might be a little more expensive if you are bold, you might go at the same price if you feel comparable, or perhaps you might price lower to gain the lower end of the market. What is missing in this decision is your own numbers for setting your costs. In some cases you don't know them yet, but for sure, following the market pricing and never revisiting it can be a problem that you may never see coming, much like my error in how many students we needed to make a room break even, let alone be profitable.

But I didn't stop there. I continued to dig. We have a crazy business model in the dance industry. We can only make money five hours out of each day between 4 and 9 p.m. We can only make money 10 months out of the year, observing holidays, because in our area, everyone wants the summer off to match the school season. There is a belief that because this is typically a hobby for our clients, they do not see it as appropriate that we make money at it. WHAT??? But those same clients still want us to be here, open in the fall, after two months of no revenue and two months of expenses, to offer classes again for five hours a day and 10 months out of the year, observing holidays, and starving over the summer. I am not aware of any other business model that says goodbye to their customers in June and folds their hands in prayer that they come back two months later. But we have done this every year for the 17 years I've owned my business, the 28 years I've been a teacher, and all my years of training leading up to being a teacher. Somehow our industry thrives, and we are here. I dug in to look at ways to ensure that we would be there every September with our smiles, greeting children who've grown so much over the summer and missed their second home.

I kept looking for the places where we could save more money that would allow me to keep my dream business and provide for my family. I took multiple seminars. I learned how to market these changes to my client families as benefits to them. I learned how discounts can slowly discount you out of business. I learned that certain types of sales strategies can devalue the product and service you are selling, rather than lift you up. I learned that a discount needs to be strategic and have something further in mind than an immediate customer. I learned that customers who only buy when there are discounts available are not my customer. I became much more aware of who my avatar really is.

How did I learn all of this? I dove straight into conferences, books, seminars, webinars, podcasts. Wherever there was learning,

I was there. Even if I had heard the speaker or topic before, I stayed present and wrote down every idea as it presented itself.

Learn who your avatar is. Mike Michalowicz taught in his book *The Pumpkin Plan* to create a "Crush and Cringe" list. This means creating a list of your customers that you just love to serve, and a list of the customers that are hard to serve. Take the customers you love and find out what makes them great, identify their features, needs, places they hang out, and then go find more of them. Once you are clear on who your ideal customer is, it is much easier to find them and then easier to say goodbye to the ones that don't meet those qualifications.

I had previously tried different marketing strategies such as Groupon-type selling, two-for-the-price-of-one programs, multiple class discounts, and discounts for multiple family members. But the truth is when you go to the grocery store, they don't discount your jug of milk because you have more people drinking it. I needed to look at my service pricing the same way.

What I serve is a want, not a need, and by understanding that my market was not everyone who might want a dance lesson, I was able to start understanding what marketing appealed to the avatar I was looking for. The people I was looking for did not want discount bargain-basement services; they wanted good-quality classrooms with highly qualified instructors, teaching safe classes within a family-friendly environment. You cannot offer those things and offer bargain-basement discounts at the same time. I started a slow shift to the type of customer that I was really looking for.

This shift was not overnight. This shift has been seven years in the making. It has been multiple small steps, incremental plans that have a four-year vision. It was never one giant leap. It has been a slow and steady vision for the company and an eye on the finances for each decision made. Along the way, I found many great resources. Most recently, I have been intently focused on a book by Mike Michalowicz called *Profit First*. His teaching in this book has been life-changing. It is giving me the ability to continue to peel back the layers and keep looking for ways to reduce the expenses and increase the profit. It is a profit that I've earned through multiple years of pouring sweat and tears and blood into my business. It is a profit I've earned by being on call 24/7 for the last 18 years. It is a profit that I have earned because there were far too many months that I did not take paycheques. It is a profit that I have earned because of the multiple things I have not been able to give my family in the past that I plan to give them in the future.

Knowing Your Numbers

Are you the type of person who checks the bank balance every day? I used to do that all the time. It is a fearful way to operate a business. I used to fear my financial statements. I cringed when I attended a workshop on finances, and I didn't know the numbers I was being asked.

- What was our total revenue?
- How much did we spend on wages?
- How much did we spend on rent or mortgage annually?
- Did I know how much a student was worth annually or lifetime?
- Did I know how much it cost to serve that student in administrative wages annually?

These are all great questions that help you figure out if your program is priced appropriately. I challenge you to ask yourself if you know the answers to some of these questions. And if you don't, commit to yourself that you will learn those numbers within the next two weeks. This will be an Action Item at the end of the chapter, but start to consider the questions now.

- Total number of customers
- Total number of units
- The amount of inventory you have at any given time: a dollar value and a quantity

- Utilization: how much of what you have available are you selling? Are you at 80%? 60%?
- How much does each customer buy monthly? Annually?
- How much is a customer worth?
- What is the lifetime value of a customer to your business if they continue to buy from you for an extended period of time?
- How many customers do you lose every year? Why?
- How many customers do you retain every year? Why?
- What is the minimum number of customers you need to stay afloat?
- What is your profit margin?
- What are your accounts receivable at any given time?
- How much does it cost to acquire a new customer?
- How much payroll does it cost to serve a customer?
- What is the true carrying cost for an employee at your company, including all benefits and taxes?
- Not all staff are equal: which of your staff is the most profitable? Which is the least?
- What are the lifetime earnings of the employees you have had with you?
- Do you have wage and raise history available to you for negotiation of new contracts?
- What is your rent-to-revenue percentage?
- What is your labour-to-revenue percentage?
- What is your year-over-year growth?
- What is your burn rate: how much does it cost just to open your doors for an hour?
- What is your gross revenue?
- What is your gross margin?

- What is your profit margin?
- How much should you be putting away for taxes? This is a normal part of doing business: be responsible and be prepared for it.
- What is your business cash position?
- How much money can you get your hands on at any given moment if you need to?
- What is your personal net worth?
- What is your business net worth?
- What is your debt-to-income ratio?

Note, this list was adapted from *More Than Just Great Dancing®! Financial Course Material*, Misty Lown.

Seven years ago, all of these questions would have made me want to lie down and close the door and never come back out again. Today I can tell you what all these numbers are within five minutes. I am not the bookkeeper; I am not the accountant. I am a responsible business owner who is taking control of what was a terrible situation, and I have righted the ship. I got myself into this mess. I got myself out through hard work and doing the things that I am not good at.

I also had no shame in hiring someone who had a skill set that was better than mine. I am an amazing dance teacher, but I had to hire out my classes so that I could focus on the things that would allow me to keep the business. To do that, I had to hire two amazing teachers to replace me and I had to be okay that they might even be better than me. By lightening my load at the business, I was able to stop working **IN** the business and start working **ON** the business.

Important Note:

When you start hiring out the jobs that you do at the studio, keep in mind how efficient you have become. It will often take a person and a half or more to replace one of the jobs that you do. Be prepared for that as you hire.

As I said, this was a series of multiple small steps. If you're feeling overwhelmed as I did, here are some quick, easy steps to get you moving in the right direction:

1. *Find a book on finances for a beginner. Learn the basic terms:*
    a. *income*
    b. *expenses*
    c. *chart of accounts,*
    d. *profit*
    e. *loss*
    f. *budget*
    g. *accounts receivable*
2. *Determine what type of accounting software suits your business best. It might be FreshBooks, QuickBooks, Simply Accounting, or an inventory program such as Zoho. It matters that you have a program that matches what you are selling.*
3. *Shop for a bookkeeper. Find someone who works well with you but who is not afraid to tell you if your spending is out of line. Interview them about their experience in your industry. How will you get information to them?*
    a. *Will they pick it up in person?*
    b. *Will you drive it to them?*
    c. *Can you email it?*
    d. *Do they have an app where you can take a picture of the receipts?*

4. *Shop for an accountant. This time we are looking for someone who is not just compliant but someone who can actually tell you if the expenditures that you have are out of line with the industry. I knew I had found this person when they first looked at my books and said, "You're paying too much in accounting fees. You're paying too much in bookkeeping fees." They had my attention; they were the first person to mention paying too much in any category, let alone their own.*

I have a mentor, Darren Hardy, who believes that the best way to become an expert in something you don't know is to decide to get the knowledge. If you truly believe that you are ready for more information about finances, look for three books, look for three seminars, three podcasts, etc. Look for a mentor in the area you wish to be smarter in. Make a concerted effort for a minimum of 30 days to immerse yourself in learning the skill that you need. Then re-evaluate. Do you need more books? Do you need to reread the same book? Do you need to pay for coaching? Do you need more podcasts? Do you need more step-by-step? Do you need hand-holding? Identify where you still need work, and do the same thing. Double down your efforts in learning what is missing. It is your responsibility as a business owner to continue to learn and grow as the global markets change.

The best money that I have spent in the past seven years has been on coaching and mentoring. I purchased a Darren Hardy program called *Insane Productivity* to help me accomplish more in a shorter period of time. I took Dave Ramsey's Financial Peace University course for my personal finances. If I couldn't do it at home with a smaller amount of money, how could I possibly expect to do more in the business with more money? I then invested in a Financial Peace Coach to get one-on-one training for my family and me. Most recently, I have invested in a Profit First coach. This one-on-one coaching has been invaluable in uncovering expenditures inside my business that I didn't even know were a problem. In the first two quarters of coaching, I have saved 23% on the expenditure side of my finances. We will continue to work over the next four quarters to get that number up closer to 50%. The best part is knowing that all those savings will drop to my bottom line personally—finally, a reward for all the hard work. Not only is it an immediate dollar amount in my pocket, but it is a security in knowing that I'm making great choices for my business to have a legacy and longevity in our community.

As my close mentor, Misty Lown, often says, "without money, there is no mission." I am endeavouring to raise tomorrow's leaders through the performing arts. It is up to me to ensure that it is profitable enough that we can show up in our community as a leader, teaching our youth how to be good stewards of the community that we leave them. I can't do this if my business fails. I put the pressure on myself to ensure this business will be a legacy, not just for my family, but for the people of my community who need better leaders who are caring and thoughtful and stewards of what we leave them. I hope that they will even improve the community we live in, not just sustain it.

Don't Bank-Bluff

Be sure that the mentor you choose to follow has the same morals and values that you do. When I purchased my third location, I did not have the money saved up for the sale. My mentor at the time taught how to "bluff" at the bank. Now, this doesn't necessarily follow my personal value system. However, I was determined to purchase this location. I don't advise the following steps because they led to financial turmoil over the next five years, and it is certainly less than honest.

I walked into the bank with a business plan for the third location, using information and financial statements from my previous two locations that were accurate and detailed. When I was turned down because my financial statements clearly showed I could not sustain another lease, or a loan and a lease, that's when I started my bluff. I told them that I had been to other banks in the area that were willing to loan the money. This was not true. I had been to no other banks. It was my hope to keep everything under one roof where I bank all my other accounts. This is where things started to get sticky. I told them the caveat set out by the other bank that was willing to loan the money was that I move all my accounts to the other branch. With this information, the loan officer gave me the money. You might think that was a success, but let me tell you why it wasn't.

1. I had not done good due diligence on the third location purchase. In fact, I had no idea how to do good diligence on that. As it turned out, we were given less than what the owner was actually selling for. I could have uncovered this with a little mentoring or learning.

2. I went in with my correct finances, and they showed that this lease and loan were not sustainable. By getting this new loan, I further tightened the noose around my own neck, ensuring that I was not getting out of my financial situation any time soon.

3. I have never lied to get where I am in business. Except for this one time, and I do believe it was the final nail in the coffin of what was my marriage. My husband at the time was not on board with the third location. I am not proud of how I obtained this money and nor am I happy with how the outcome went. I spent many years trying to untangle the web of a location I should never have purchased.

The moral of the story is that if you shouldn't have it, do the right work and the right due diligence to put yourself in a position to be ready for it when the time is right next time around.

Keep Personal and Business Apart

When I started my business, my dad had recently retired from his years working as an auditor for a large department store. At first, having his help was a blessing. But it soon turned into a repeat of terrible nights of high school math homework, where we fought over how it was best to be done and with different ways of how to do it. As an auditor, he naturally was looking for every single penny. I, as an artist, was naturally looking for a quick solution that would get me back to the classroom and back to the creative side of the business. Multiple times I pulled the missing cents out of my purse and put them on the desk and said, "Can we be finished now"? But as I now know, I did not pick up the lessons he was trying to tell me. What he couldn't say was, or perhaps I was unwilling to hear, "You don't know what I'm trying to tell you and it is really important." As he was older and risk was no longer part of his portfolio, I made an assumption that he just didn't understand what I was trying to do. The lesson I missed is that just because he was afraid of risk didn't mean that his input wasn't extremely valuable to the function of our business.

The moral of the story: pulling money out of your wallet to balance your books is not the answer. You need a deeper understanding if you are going to be successful.

Don't Wait for Luck

Seven years of doing the right work, the hard work, the unsexy work of bookkeeping led me to be prepared for an amazing opportunity. Because that's what it is; it is not "luck." When opportunity meets preparation, it can look like "luck" on the outside, but from the inside, I knew that I deserved this opportunity. I had made the decision to close two out of three locations upon separating from my husband. It was hard to wrap my ego around the choice for success with one location, then to go down with the ship and my ego on three locations. I had bided my time over seven years, and finally, the opportunity presented itself. In our condominiumized commercial building, the unit beside us came up for sale and I had done enough work on my finances to be able to qualify to purchase that unit based on my own merits. Me, the single mom with $0.29 in the bank eight years ago, living cheque to cheque, using Pinterest to make the ice in my deep freeze look like dinner, was in a position to own more than 1.2 million in commercial real estate! Those who know me know that that was not "luck" at all. I walked into the bank proudly with my financial statements and no stories about going elsewhere for the funding, just me and my hard work, and a stamp of approval. I can tell you that that mortgage was much more satisfying than the loan for my third location that I had gotten with less than savoury conduct.

The moral of the story: work hard and when opportunity meets preparation, you are ready for the "luck" at hand.

Action Item: Crush and Cringe List (Mike Michalowicz)

This means creating a list of your customers that you just love to serve, and a list of the customers that are hard to serve. Take the customers you love and find out what makes them great, identify their features, needs, and places they hang out, and then go find more of them.

Action Item: Finances

Take a moment to look up these figures.

- *What is your total revenue for your fiscal year?*
- *How much did you spend on wages?*
- *How much did you spend on rent or mortgage annually?*
- *How much is a client worth annually or lifetime?*
- *How much does it cost to serve that client in administrative wages annually?*
- *Total number of customers*
- *Total number of units*
- *The amount of inventory you have at any given time: a dollar value and a quantity*
- *Utilization: how much of what you have available are you selling? Are you at 80%? 60%?*
- *How much does each customer buy monthly? Annually?*
- *How much is a customer worth?*
- *What is the lifetime value of a customer to your business if they continue to buy from you for an extended period of time?*
- *How many customers do you lose every year? Why?*
- *How many customers do you retain every year? Why?*
- *What is the minimum number of customers you need to stay afloat?*
- *What is your profit margin?*
- *What are your accounts receivable at any given time?*
- *How much does it cost to acquire a new customer?*
- *How much payroll does it cost to serve a customer?*

- *What is the true carrying cost for an employee at your company, including all benefits and taxes?*
- *Not all staff are equal. Which of your staff is the most profitable? Which is the least?*
- *What are the lifetime earnings of the employees you have had with you?*
- *Do you have wage and raise history available to you for negotiation of new contracts?*
- *What is your rent-to-revenue percentage?*
- *What is your labour-to-revenue percentage?*
- *What is your year-over-year growth?*
- *What is your burn rate: how much does it cost just to open your doors for an hour?*
- *What is your gross revenue?*
- *What is your gross margin?*
- *What is your profit margin?*
- *How much should you be putting away for taxes? This is a normal part of doing business: be responsible and be prepared for it.*
- *What is your business cash position?*
- *How much money can you get your hands on at any given moment if you need it to?*
- *What is your personal net worth?*
- *What is your business net worth?*
- *What is your debt-to-income ratio?*

Note that this list was adapted from *More Than Just Great Dancing®! Financial Course Material*, Misty Lown.

CHAPTER 5 – STAFFING

Only you can take responsibility for your happiness. . . but you can't do it alone. It's the great paradox of being human.

Simon Sinek

You can't do it alone if you wish to build a legacy.

Let's start with how I ended up with my first few employees. I think we all do something similar when we are getting started. We tap the relationships we already have, and that tends to be friends and family at the start. The problem with friends and family is that typically they always believe they're doing you a favour even though you are writing a paycheque. The power differential in a situation like this does not allow for an employee or family or friend to grow. Relationships such as these typically end in a negative manner with both parties feeling unappreciated. It is rare that these relationships stay positive. **The truth is that the people you start your business with are not the people you're going to finish with**. People do not grow at the same rate; they grow differently for different reasons. You will need different people for different seasons in your company. This gives way to the idea that you might need to advertise to find your next round of employees to take you to the next place.

I, like others, hired family and friends to help lift my business off the ground in its initial phase. I struggled to provide constructive feedback, which now looks like it should have been an employee review that was formalized. At that time, I had nothing in place to review performance in the workplace. I needed to spend some time creating a system for that. When someone feels like they're doing you a favour, it's difficult to accept any kind of constructive feedback. This led to multiple staff making me feel like I was hostage to the people I was paying. I struggled to be able to change behaviour, ask for more, or ask for something different. There were many people doing it how they wanted to do it, and they weren't interested in changing. We will talk more about this type of employee later in other chapters. I now know they were mercenaries.

When you know better you do better.

- Maya Angelou

Now that I know better, I can look back on the type of manager that I was at the start. I did not have enough leadership skills for the volume of people and the task at hand. I was also hiring people who were young in the industry and expecting them to be able to fill in what I didn't know. I can see now that it was an unrealistic expectation to think that someone who is equally as young in the industry as I was would have any better leadership skills than myself. It was a recipe for eventual disaster. As I grew my company and my leadership skills, I began to look for people outside of my friends and family circle.

It took me many years to realize what skills I was missing and to seek out mentorship and education to become a better leader. Leadership is like that: it is ever-changing, and it is a commitment to always be growing and being honest with your team.

Servant leadership puts the focus on the community in which the person serves. All actions are intended to improve the lives of others. There is a shared power, as the needs and development of others are the primary focus.

Typical leadership has the focus on whoever the top of the organizational chart might be. There is a focus of power to one person, and it is accumulated rather than shared.

Being a leader means allowing your team to accept the accolades for a job well done and falling on your own sword when something doesn't go well for the whole team. That means that a leader never takes credit for any jobs well done. They always point to the team that made it happen. It takes a lot of maturity and understanding of relationships to get to a place where people see you as a true leader. **The only evidence of leadership is that you leave leaders behind you.**

As I grew my company and my leadership skills (slowly), I began to look for employees outside of my friends and family circle. This wasn't necessarily as successful as I had hoped it would be because now I was hiring the friends of friends. I had not cast my net wide enough yet at this point. I was throwing bodies at positions during a time when the industry was booming, and it was difficult to find the quality of teacher that I was hoping for. This led to another couple of years of employees that were not living up to what I had hoped for when I hired them. I cannot emphasize enough how important it is to attract and hire the right people.

This has given me way too many years of training on how to hire and how to lead a team. You can learn to be a leader. You can learn the skills you need to lead in a variety of ways. Over the years, many workshops and conferences have helped me identify the type of leadership that is most natural to me. The system we now have in place ensures that only the right people are being let through to the interview process. I encourage you to look at your hiring process and determine if it is serving you.

How to Hire the Right Staff

The moment you feel the need to tightly manage someone, you have made a hiring mistake. The best people don't need to be managed. Guided, taught, led – yes. But not tightly managed.

James C. Collins

We often only hire people who mirror us. Not just the people who say we are nice or that our outfit looks great, but people who think the same as we do or behave the same way that we do. This is a natural attraction to someone who is similar to us. They think the same way, making them easy to get along with. This doesn't necessarily lead to success in staffing. Often we need to be hiring someone who is the opposite of us. Someone who has the skill set that we are missing. In my organization, we often refer to the visionary as the kite and the director/managers as the string. All organizations need someone who is in a visionary leadership role, and all organizations need employees who will complete the vision down to all the small details to ensure it's done correctly and completely. This means you need to put a hiring process in place that will prevent you from hiring more visionaries, to protect you from hiring more people like you, and to help you hire more people who are not like you to help complete the vision.

This looks like asking for resumes and cover letters with certain details right from the start. We ask for specific things: I want to know that they pay attention to detail and timelines from the start. Asking them to fill in a Google form that has a few more questions that help us understand who they are and why they're applying. This form has paragraph answers, which allows us to see what their written communication looks like. Step three is for them to provide us with a video of why they want to work for us. If they do not complete these three steps in a timely manner, they do not even receive an interview. It is fascinating what people believe is appropriate for cover letters. Did they personalize it for the job, or are they mass applying? I want someone who pays attention to what they are applying for. The most important thing is the video. They could record this video as many times as they wish, they could wear whatever they think is appropriate, and they could also use whatever background they think is relevant. It is fascinating what people believe is fitting as a submission. However, when people are applying for a job, they are on their best behaviour, and if their first indication is these three steps and that is their best behaviour, you now know if you need to continue with the rest of the process.

When someone shows you who they are, believe them the first time.

Maya Angelou

I have had videos submitted from people standing in loud, busy hair salons. I have had a video submitted from inside someone's front hall closet, wearing their children's winter hat with a flashlight under their chin while they whispered. I had a mom in her pyjamas with her two-year-old banging her on the head with a toy as a video submission. I've also had wonderful submissions sitting on living room couches with wonderful sayings on walls behind them, beautifully edited with additional music, and wonderful submissions of why they would be a rock star for my company. It's important to note that in a process where they can record it over and over, you should pay attention to what they think is appropriate and may not be appropriate. If that person is meant to be your front line, your reception, the first face of your company that people see, it's important that they understand about first impressions. The noisy hair salon video makes me ask why was that the location for the video? The flashlight video tells me they may not be taking this seriously. The toddler with the toy and pyjamas makes me ask what prevented you from waiting until nap time and getting yourself dressed before filming? On the contrary, the beautiful videos with edits show me they care, they take pride in their work, and this is important enough to take some extra time to stand out. The single addition of the video submission to our hiring process has helped us sidestep several bad hires. Often when we post on online job sites, we end up with multiple applications from around the world for a part-time position. We are not in a position to be bringing people into the country through immigration for work. It's important to have some of these things in place to save yourself time and the headache of wading through multiple applications that are just not eligible. This has saved me thousands of hours in wasted interview times. I don't even look at any applications unless they submit a video. At that point, I will review things they have submitted up to then, including cover letter, resume, Google form, and video. I'll determine if they get more of my time for an interview. I am also watching how long it took them to complete the three steps. How badly do they want this? Is it a priority for them?

Bad Hires Cost the Company

Human resources isn't a thing we do. It is the thing that runs the business.

Steve Wynn

According to a survey conducted by Career Builder, companies lose an average of $15,000 on every bad hire. Even worse, that number only goes up as the salary of the worker increases.

The training cost, the cost of poor customer service, the cost of lost customers, lost team morale – the list goes on. It is really important to have a great hiring practice that is proven. That provides staff throughout the year. That allows you to put the right person in the right position rather than making "panic hires." Many of us fail to let someone go because we do not have a replacement available. Run ads all year long, and allow people to deselect themselves through the process to lessen the time investment. Conduct interviews only when the right people come along, and keep their applications at the ready should a position open up or a need arise. Hiring is difficult and painful, but it is a requirement. It should not be something you do once in a while. It should be an ongoing process.

Having great people inside your company is the single hardest task to complete. It took us more than 15 years to get to a place where we attract the type of employee that we have been looking for. We have now built ourselves a reputation in the community for being a place that hires and acts upon servant leadership principles. Now when people are asked why they want to work for us, we are getting answers such as, "I have seen you in the community and appreciate what you are doing," "I really identify with your mission," "I am looking for a company that wants to make a difference." Previous submissions were people who were just looking for a job, and we're not necessarily on the mission that we were on.

In the early days, when I had three locations and I had multiple staff at each location to manage, I had started to use Skype as an interview tool. At that point in time, I was overwhelmed from a time management perspective and thought that I was clever by using technology. This technology is amazing and can be awesome when used in the right way. I, however, chose to use it as a hiring tool to save me the time of driving to interviews and all of my locations. There were times when I interviewed potential staff via Skype and hired them, and they worked for me for an entire year, and I never met them face to face. That's how overwhelmed I was with my scheduling. Now, these people were decent teachers, they did a good job, but I think we can agree that they were not necessarily engaged staff when they never met their boss, and they never had face-to-face time with their leader. The embarrassing part of this is that if I met them on the street or at an event, I would never recognize the people who were hired in this way, yet I provided them with a paycheque for a full year. They worked for my company for a full year! This is a really crazy experience for a small business. There is a time and a place for technology, and it can be useful, but it cannot replace face-to-face relationships.

There is a lot of concern about teachers teaching at multiple locations for different owners and sharing company secrets in the process. The truth is that most of us are running our studios in similar ways and we need similar people. We are all looking for great teachers with good hearts, who care about the development of their students. The delivery of the product is what sets us apart. That delivery is your mission and your vision.

Hire Slow and Fire Fast

When I had three locations, I identified the need to hire a really good right-hand person. This was the first time I had set out to hire a salary position inside my company. I was looking for a specific individual. I needed someone who could teach as well as or better than I could. I also needed someone who had great attention to detail. Someone who was interested in the inner workings of the business but not interested in starting their own business. In our industry, this is a tall order. I placed an ad in November, and lo and behold, the most amazing application came in!

When I interviewed this person, she was employed by a local competitor. She was interested in the full-time salary position and was hoping to start as soon as possible. The hard part for me was that I wanted someone who wasn't going to leave me mid-season. For her to start with me as soon as possible would be for her to leave someone else mid-season. At this point, I had learned that **if they'll do it to someone else, they will do it to you.** I made a scary ask. I asked her to complete her contract with her current employer and that I would hire her at the end of the season. To my surprise, that is exactly what she did. She completed her contract with grace, and she worked with her employer at that time to exit properly. And to date, she has been one of my best hires and continues to be my right-hand person, going on eight years now. **Make the hard ask, learn their character, and find out if they are right for your company.**

When Should You Fire Someone?

The first time you think about it. Of course, hiring staff is no bed of roses. There's always someone that you need to exit, or my favourite phrase, "release them to the competition." As all businesses do, I've had my ups and downs with employees who have left. In our industry, it's not uncommon for teachers to leave and attempt to lure students to their new place of work, be it a new place that they are teaching or a new business if they have opened themselves. I did experience this in its most devastating fashion not too long ago.

This particular employee had been with me for six years. I had taken her on as a high-level employee. She had access to all the inner parts of the business. I had paid for her to go to multiple conferences and take a lot of training. Once we had taken on the third location, there was a lot more financial pressure on the company to make things work. This employee did not take kindly to the demands that I made on her time and how the company needed to best use her skills for the success of the mission. It was clear that she was unhappy and that we would be in our last season together. We spent months walking on eggshells around each other.

I knew that she needed to go, I knew we were no longer on the same mission, but I did not have the tools in place or the access to higher-level instructors to replace her. She should have been let go, but instead I kept her for eight months longer than I should have – eight months! Eight months of access to student records, client lists, company policies, training methods, vendor relationships, and on and on. The results of not being prepared to replace a staff member were devastating.

She chose to open her own business and lured away the majority of one of my programs, resulting in the loss of $100,000 in sales in one single year. Many people asked me, "Did you have a non-compete clause in place?" The answer is yes, I did. It's not enough to have it in place, you have to be willing to spend the money legally to fight it. And at the end of the day, if you win, what do you really win? The clients are unlikely to return and the person you are fighting may not be able to pay the judgment. This decision to not let her go when I knew it was time was one of the costliest mistakes I have made in my business. The $100,000 was a single-year loss, and the lifespan of a student in my company is seven years. The compound loss could be calculated at $700,000+. And never mind all the other impacts this person had on my business.

The majority of the contracts we have had in place with our staff are largely unenforceable. I learned the many mistakes of not recording disciplinary action and corrective-action conversations properly. It is virtually impossible to fire someone for cause at this point in time in the society we live in. It is much easier to pay someone out to leave when they are no longer a good fit for your company. When there's not much money inside your business, it feels difficult to pay someone out to make them go away. However, in my experience, the expense of allowing someone to stay when they should be gone is too great. You can't afford to let them stay. Someone who does not belong with your company anymore can do so much damage. They can sway clients. They can steal company secrets. They can poach company processes, vendor relationships, and other staff. It is difficult to put a dollar value on an employee who is no longer on the same mission as you.

I have also dealt with employee theft. This taught me to inspect what I expect when doing payroll and time sheets. I'd had 15 years of employees who had been honest. It never occurred to me that this could happen inside my own company. In this particular case, the employee had started to book the wrong wage code early on in their employment. Each paycheque, they used the wrong pay code for a few more hours, until eventually they had lifted more than $10,000 in overpayments for work, in little over a year. I now pay much closer attention to payroll. We are also looking at ways to ensure payroll theft is not possible. I encourage you to also look at your systems and processes to see where there may be holes.

There are many ways to ensure that your payroll stays controlled. Use an online payroll company. They have sophisticated tracking and reporting that will allow you to see trends and one-offs when they happen. There are various pay rates with my employees, and tracking those hours can sometimes be time-consuming. Consider a time-card reader. They are no longer the old-school punch-card systems; they read thumbprints and scan people in and out at various pay rates for various tasks. You can pre-code the hours employees can work, and outside of those hours approval is required before they can be recorded.

When I was faced with closing two of my three locations, I had 27 staff members at that time. It was an incredibly heart-wrenching decision as to who would keep their job and who would be released to the workforce. I had a lot of thinking to do about what type of company I really wanted to have and which of these employees were the ones who were going to get us there.

At the time, I had heard a teaching from Steve Chandler about **Patriots versus Mercenaries.** Patriots are the employees who are on the same mission as you. They love what they do, they are servant-leadership-driven, they are proud and committed to the company and the values in place. But most importantly, they are driven to ensure that the mission and vision are at the forefront of their work. Mercenaries are employees who are there for the paycheque and the personal glory. They are not team players, they tend to break the rules, they tend to do things and ask for forgiveness after. And they are not concerned about their choices and their interactions and how they affect the other employees. They're there for their personal glory.

After hearing this teaching and looking at my staff list, it became clear which seven employees would stay on and which ones would be released back to the workforce. With the closing of two locations, and the shedding of employees who are not necessarily on the same mission as me, came the ability to really become a great leader and cast the vision that I had always wanted. While it was devastating to tell 20 people that I did not have room for them on my team, the seven that I handpicked were amazing, and I can honestly say this was a turning point for the business. I had never been in a position of overstaffing before. We were always throwing bodies at jobs. We were always hoping that the right person would come through the door. This time we had enough to choose from to properly staff our needs. **We were in a position to place tasks with talent.**

Outsourcing

Another option to solve staffing issues is outsourcing. Many small businesses do not have the capacity to hire part-time workers for many of the things that you need. Outsourcing looks like your bookkeeper, a graphics artist, a lawyer to help you with your contracts and policies, a human resources expert to help you write your employee handbook and to deal with difficult situations. Outsourcing can be useful in determining whether you need to hire the person in-house or if it can continue to be a contractor to your business.

I continue to do a lot of outsourcing now, even as we have grown a bit larger again with 15 employees. Outsourcing continues to be one of the most cost-effective routes we have available to us when embarking on new projects or determining if the project needs to be brought in-house. It continues to be a great way to relieve pressure during certain times of the year when there is more work to be done than there are hours. It allows us to gain the extra manpower required without overloading my current team.

There are often discussions in our industry about employees versus contractors. I think when we're talking about outsourcing, it is a great time to talk about what makes an employee and what makes a contractor. Contractors can be thought of as the painter that you hire. They will tell you when they are available and what products they will use, and they provide their own equipment and will show up on their own schedule. This works if you agree to their terms.

An employee is someone who is provided with the equipment by the company, and they are told when to show up, who they will do it with, and how they will do the work. If you are not sure if an employee or a contractor is right for you, I can help you make that determination. I often consult with businesses short term to help them clean up their systems. For me, it would be a huge problem if a teacher decided when they were going to teach, what they were going to teach, and who they were going to teach it to. It matters to me that they show up on time every time and deliver the products that we are promising, which is a great dance lesson of the type we sold for that time slot to that age, and use the tools that I have provided, teaching the clients that I am providing. It would not serve my clients well if teachers showed up when they wanted to and used whatever tools they felt were appropriate. For us, all of my people are employees. **I want to be able to set the parameters around their employment and around their payment.** To do that, they must be employees.

Benefits

That leads me to my next topic, which is providing employee benefits. As employees, my staff receive the benefit of employer-matched Employment Insurance and employer-sponsored pension plan insurance. These are a requirement of our Canadian government. We often talk about how Canada has an amazing maternity leave program. Employees who pay into Employment Insurance have access to these paid maternity plans through this benefit. As a business that employs largely young women, this is a great benefit to the majority of people I hire.

As an employer, I feel **it is important to show my employees that I care about their future and their families.** Employees who have been with me for a predetermined length of time and have worked a certain number of hours a week also have access to additional benefits. We have a health benefit plan that provides additional care for the employee and their family. This is an employer matching program, where they pay 50% of the cost and I match 50% of the cost. We also have an Employee Retirement Savings Program. The same employees who have access to the health benefit plan due to the length of time working and the number of hours per week also have access to this Retirement Savings Plan. It is also an employer match, meaning that if an employee puts in $50, I will match it $50 and they will have $100 going into their Retirement Savings Plan per month.

It is important to invest in your staff if you want them to grow and become part of your legacy. Good people are worth the investment. As I mentioned earlier, keeping a poor staff person has a huge consequence on your bottom line in multiple ways. Keeping a great staff person also has a huge consequence to your bottom line, but in this case, it is always positive. Be sure to look after your staff, be sure that they feel seen and important. **Someone who feels appreciated will always do more than is expected of them.**

Action Item: How to Hire the Right Staff

What is your hiring system?
- *Write down all the steps currently in place.*
- *How can you add steps that help candidates deselect themselves, such as a form to fill in or a task to do prior to the interview? This helps reduce the number of interviews you will have to do.*
- *Can you add another person or two to the process to help you make the decision on hires?*

Action Item: Bad Hires

According to Gallup, in 2017, at any point, 73% of your team is not on the same mission as you and may be actively working against you.
- *Who on your team is underperforming?*
- *Can they be retrained?*
- *Should they be let go?*

Review your system for performance reviews.
- *Do you have a system?*
- *How frequently do employees get feedback?*
- *How frequently do they have the opportunity to give you feedback?*

Action Item: Outsourcing

What jobs are you doing that could be outsourced?
- *Cleaning*
- *Graphic design*
- *Data entry*
- *Bookkeeping*
- *Accounting*
- *Social media*

The list is endless in possibilities. Make a list of the top three things to outsource, and commit to a date to make it happen.

Action Item: Benefits

Do you have benefits that your employees could partake in? Make a list of what you could offer.

- *Financial*
- *Health benefits*
- *Retirement*
- *Daycare*
- *Tuition*
- *Sick leave*
- *Vacation days*
- *Etc.*

CHAPTER 6 – SYSTEMS

Systems run the business and people run the systems.

Michael E. Gerber

Overloaded and so very broken. This is how I began to feel a few years into business. So many things were being done the hard way, reactionary instead of proactive. By hand and as I remembered, forgetting important steps along the way, oftentimes repeating mistakes I had already learned from because I did not document or build a system as I went. It was exhausting, knowing that a mistake was coming—it was just a matter of when.

According to Studio Owner University®, in the dance industry, your systems will break with every grouping of 250 students enrolled. Every single system—your database, your policies, your hiring, your firing, your methodology—all of it. Broke down, rusted, straight worn out, busted. Too many students, not enough structure, too many staff, not enough leadership, not enough patriots to help carry the mission. Not enough time to repeat the mission clearly and frequently. Whatever it is will break, and you need to be preparing for the next system that will not be robust enough for your growth.

There I was, no support at home, no way to shut off work, and my network was not strong enough to provide the support I needed. Business became everything—it was all I could think about, eat, sleep, and talk about. This was where every trap I could fall into was strapped like dynamite to my heart and to my business. My lack of understanding of systems was almost a kryptonite. It was dragging me under, and I had no idea what the problem was. I just knew that I was the only one who could fix it because I was the only one who "knew" everything. And that was my biggest problem.

Systems are so important to our business. I used to think systems were big, onerous, cumbersome entities. Something with hundreds, if not thousands, of steps, that had a massive manual and was impossible for a small business like me to create on my own. The truth is that a system is simply a set of steps or progressions to complete something repeatedly. Your business should have systems for everything, big or small:

- Opening for the day
- Closing for the day
- Cashing out sales
- Issuing payroll
- Bank deposits

The list is endless for the systems you need to create and document. I refer to the documentation of all systems as the **"Hit-by-a-Bus Plan." All businesses need one.** This is the operations manual that will allow the business to continue in the case of your absence, planned or otherwise.

The intention is to create a business model where the owner does not have all the details and staff are able to execute day-to-day functions so that the business owner is no longer working in the business, but instead they are freed up to work on the business.

The reason you need a hit-by-a-bus plan in your business is that it's not about if you will be out of the business; it is when. Most of the time, you won't get to choose when that happens; the universe will choose for you. When that happens, ensure you have done the work so your business can carry on in your absence. Some of these absences can be more than a couple of weeks, so this planning is key.

Many business owners end up working inside of their business instead of on their businesses, especially in the first years of the start-up. Often neglected in this situation is the practice of writing down the systems built because you are too ingrained in the day-to-day operations. It doesn't occur to you that you will need to write it down, allowing someone else to carry it forward in your absence. You might have even told yourself that you are too busy to record it and you will get to it later. **This is your reminder that later never comes.** And once you have been called away, it will be too late to get those systems recorded.

Anxiety is the gap between now and later.

Frederick Salomon Perls

I had been working on my hit-by–a-bus plan for more than three years when I needed to execute it. My dad became terribly ill. My "why" is my family, and if my business does not allow me to show up for them when they need me, then what is the purpose of being in charge? I was able to step back from the business and be with my dad for the last five months of his life. To navigate the doctor appointments and help my mom care for him, giving him the opportunity to stay home as long as possible, which was his final wish, to be in the comfort of his own home as long as possible. He managed to stay home until the last week of his life when we had to take him to hospice because his needs were beyond our ability.

The ability to spend those final months with him was beyond words precious to me. We were able to have the deep conversations that we sometimes neglect to have when things are good. We learned more about each other in the final months than we did the previous 10 years. I learned of his deep strength and was brought to my knees many times by his love for Mom, unwavering and devoted up until his last breath. I witnessed so many precious moments that still play vividly in my mind today. I will never regret the time spent away from my business to have these incredible loving experiences. The time to sit quietly and provide conversation, levity, or just plain honest truths. This gift of time brings me peace today and a perspective that I would otherwise have missed in the business of entrepreneurship.

In my absence, my business persisted on one time block in the morning between 5:30 and 7:00 am. I then spent the rest of my day where I was needed, at my parents' side. My team knew what they needed to do and were able to carry on all activities without skipping a beat. Even more surprisingly, we experienced 10% growth that season when I stepped back and allowed the team the opportunity to grow into the training and skills I had provided. When I returned to the company, I experienced another phenomenon – they no longer needed me in the same way. I had worked my way out of my own company.

Let's talk about how to build systems that will allow businesses to operate in the owner's absence, as well as systems that will allow the training of staff to be more effective and more successful.

Building a Dream Team

If you hire people just because they can do a job, they'll work for your money. But if you hire people who believe what you believe, they'll work for you with blood and sweat and tears.

Simon Sinek

Does this sound familiar?

You receive a resume, or a person walks into your business looking for work. You schedule an interview; you have a list of questions that you think are pretty good. The person shows up reasonably interested, checks most of the boxes, and you think you can train what they lack. You leave the interview dreaming of how this person will lighten your workload and help you move forward. They show up, and it's a lot of work to get them up to speed.

You don't have a real list of everything they need to know, so training is spotty and not very strong. Then they start to disappoint you with not meeting the expectations you never laid out clearly or training you never gave. Before you know it, you both dislike the relationship, and it's quickly becoming difficult to work together. You never see completely eye to eye. Tasks never seem to get finished to your satisfaction, so you start to take them back on again, this time with resentment in your heart and mind because this person was supposed to make things better, and they aren't. Then you start to think this person is not as good as they said they were, you spend several weeks trying to decide what to do, then they give notice, and you are in crisis because you don't have any other bandwidth available to cover them, and they leave. You panic and take everything back onto your own plate, and you start the cycle all over again.

I know many of you are nodding that you have had this experience, or maybe you are living it now. **Stop the cycle! It costs your business so much in money and team morale, including yours!**

I used to just hope that another person would come along and apply for a job with me. This person would care as much as I did, see the business the way I did, and want to operate the same way I did. I spent years being disappointed by the people I hired. **No one will ever care about your business more than you do unless they have skin in the game**. Your magical employee will not appear out of the sky until you get ready for their arrival. This preparation is lots of hard work and system building. You have to build the systems so that someone else can do them. Someone else can train on them and refer to it for clarification and refreshing, especially tasks that are infrequent.

Hiring people is an art, not a science, and resumes can't tell you whether someone will fit into a company's culture.

Howard Schultz

Many business owners are waiting for their dream team to appear: They are waiting for the right candidate to walk through the doors – that person who just "gets it." This is also the biggest lie that owners tell themselves because that dream team is not going to magically appear. You are going to have to build it yourself, person by person. Let's get to work!

One of the most valuable changes that I made to my business recently was through the More Than Just Great Dancing®! Executive Program. In the full-day training, we explored the three constructs of service and how they run through our tuition-based businesses. It is true, and it works. Let's start with acknowledging the main three constructs of your team inside your business. Those three pieces are:

1. Sales: Administration
2. Service: Teachers
3. Support: Leadership

These three pieces often overlap, which can confuse your team as to which position they are in and what they are responsible for. The overlap happens because many of your team players sit in multiple seats, and job descriptions and roles need to be clearly defined for a team to see advancement. Oftentimes leaders begin placing people into positions because the work needs to get done, and in the chaos, the full job description never becomes realized. **This "throwing bodies at jobs" almost always ends in disappointment for everyone involved.** A company on a growth trajectory needs a better plan and a formula for success!

It's common for leaders to wait too long to hire someone, leading to a rushed hire that ends up with fragmented and incomplete training, which in turn frustrates both you and them.

This is a cycle too, one that you can easily find yourself in without even realizing the harmful outcomes to your team morale and the bottom line. Bad hires are expensive, but what is even more costly is a poor hiring system that perpetuates bad hiring.

Break the cycle and build a triumphant dream team that will sell, serve, and support with clear roles and expectations.

When Is It Time to Restructure Your Team

There are many ways to look at the structure of your team. Your team is also fluid. As your company grows, so do your team and its assets. How do you know when it is time to restructure?

1. When what you're doing doesn't work anymore
    a. This is the most common reason business owners make changes!
2. In anticipation of growth
    a. This is the least common reason but the best choice for a healthy organization.

1. When what you're doing doesn't work anymore

There are multiple reasons why staffing and job descriptions no longer work; the most common are listed below. Once you identify your situation, the solution becomes clearer.

A. Problem: Too much work and not enough people
Solution: Hire from the outside

When there is too much work and not enough people, you need to hire from outside the organization to solve the problem, instead of overloading your staff. You decide what the position is, what skills are needed, and then advertise and fill the role. Take the time to consult the existing team and talk about the skill set that is missing and the tasks that need a champion. This is how you can start to build the job description. Then before you run off to place an ad or start interviewing, think about the attributes the ideal person has—more on this in a future chapter.

I had a client, David, who ran a large performing arts school, who understood that he needed to hire. His team was stretched thin, and everyone was regularly booking overtime. There was too much work, and he just wanted to get that ad out and bring in someone quickly to help. I encouraged him to pause and take time to write out a list of tasks and areas where his team was weak and he needed to hire a certain skill set to fill in the gaps. I also suggested he speak to his team about what they saw as the skills they needed in order to be better. By being thoughtful about the skills his team needed to reach the next level, he was able to be smart about the type of hire he made and the expectations under which that person was hired. He was also able to ensure the ad spoke to the type of person they really needed.

If he had not taken that time, it is possible he would not have hired the skills he needed and may have made a bad hire or hired for skills his team already had. In this case, he was surprised to learn what skills his team wanted him to hire for. By taking their input, he was able to ensure they were moving in the right direction for success.

B. Problem: Blurry lines across positions
Solution: Redefine job descriptions

When there are blurry lines and people on your team are not sure who's in charge of what, you need to redefine their job descriptions. Your team deserves to know exactly what their job entails and what success in their position looks like. That starts with understanding exactly what is expected of them. Gather the department and understand what they are all doing now, and what is and is not in their job description. Look at what tasks are outside of the role and discuss if adding them in is the right thing for the company. If not, add it to the above list of *Too much work and not enough people*, and contemplate the type of person you need to hire for success in those tasks.

In my company, we often had several part-time employees working our front desk in the evenings. We had a bank of tasks that fell under "front desk," and it was expected that they would get done during the shift they worked. However, some tasks were far too big to finish in a shift, and they would not get picked up by the next person who came in. So many things went unfinished and things began to fall apart.

After a period of time, we were able to see that even within a position, we still needed to assign tasks to individuals to ensure they would get seen through efficiently to the end. By clearing up who was responsible for what, even within a position where everyone was responsible for the tasks, we were able to ensure tasks were completed.

C. Problem: Right bus, wrong seat

But I know this much: If we get the right people on the bus, the right people in the right seats, and the wrong people off the bus, then we will figure out how to take it some place great.

Jim Collins

Solution: Redistribute the workload

Jim Collins was the first to bring forward this concept of seats on the bus. In fact, he wrote a whole book on it: *Good to Great*. If someone's on the right bus (they have the right character traits for your company) but in the wrong seat (they're in a position that's not the best fit), then that means you can redistribute work to the right people. To do this, you're going to evaluate your team's skills and interests and raise up current people who are already inside your culture. The bonus of this is that you already have great people who want to grow with you – use them!

A client of mine, Amelia, who ran a successful clothing store, had to rearrange seats on the bus. At my direction, in a staff meeting, she wrote out all the jobs on cue cards and laid them out on the table. The staff each took the ones that they were responsible for. There were still a large number of cards left on the table. Those in attendance asked about the cards left over. "Those are the tasks that I am responsible for," said Amelia.

She then said, "Put back any cards you don't want to be responsible for, that are not your skill set, or you just do not get excited about the task." After the cards had been returned, she took mental note of what cards each person had returned to the table. Then she instructed them to pick up any cards for tasks they were excited about or felt were a better match for their skill set. This is where the magic happened.

Two of her employees completely switched roles. They actually gave each other their entire job descriptions! They swapped roles and job descriptions. Lo and behold, things improved dramatically overnight for this company and its ability to get things done. Right bus, wrong seat.

D. Problem: Wrong bus
Solution: It's time to part ways

If someone is on the wrong bus altogether, meaning they are simply not a good fit for your company, then you need to release them to the competition. When should you fire someone? The first time you think of it. If you wait, the cost to your business can be catastrophic.

Another coaching client of mine, Kathryn, who runs a dance school, had a couple of teachers on staff who were very clearly mercenaries. She knew it too. But she had convinced herself that they could be coached into better ways, or "Just get to the end of the contract, I don't have replacements..." I think we all know what the list of excuses can look like. But she waited too long to make the call to remove them from her team. In the meantime, the two staff members managed to create enough trouble in her whole team to cause substantial damage to the company's reputation. The teachers began to make even the good employees question the leadership and policies. They spoke to customers about moving their business elsewhere – to the company they would be working at in the future. The damage was lengthy and definitely hurt the bottom line. It took several months to uncover all the ways that these two employees caused issues inside the business. The bottom line is that you have to fire fast.

Dealing with employee issues can be difficult, but not dealing with them can be worse.

Paul Foster

---

2. Anticipation of Growth

When possible, the best time to hire or move people on your team is when you are anticipating growth. Healthy things grow, and you should always be looking for the next level of growth that your company can sustain. When setting growth goals, you should also be mindful of what has to happen to the roles in your organizational structure to sustain that achievement.

To plan for growth there are a few steps you can follow to set up your team for success:

1. Outline your growth goals – clear, concise, measurable, time-stamped. A growth goal might consist of specific enrollment milestones, revenue percentages, or an increase in units (classes) per student.
2. Assess what structure is needed inside your organization to support that growth. The structure includes your organizational chart and how many hours a week each person works on which task. You might ask yourself questions like: Are there people who have room for more work inside their available hours? Who does each person report to? Are there cross-training opportunities?

3. Take measure of your hiring protocol to ensure you are bringing in the best candidates. Review the protocol to ensure you don't waste time with inappropriate applications or candidates who aren't a good culture fit. Build an interview procedure that weeds those people out before too much time is spent.

4. Evaluate your training procedures to ensure your training budget is spent wisely. Are procedures clearly written for your new hire? Is it clear what successful training looks like? Have a plan to bring them into your company culture and develop 30, 60, and 90 day goals for training milestones.

If you want to sustain longevity and healthy growth inside your organization, you need to plan for the growth and grow each position before it's in crisis.

Building a dream team takes planning, consideration, and, most of all, a growth mindset. Dream teams don't just happen; they grow. Plan for growth, then work the plan!

Scheduling

> *The key is not to prioritize what's on your schedule, but to schedule your priorities.*
>
> *Stephen Covey*

I used to say that plans were for pansies. As an artist, I felt that scheduling my day or week would cramp my ability to create. I used to let my wild mind decide what was important each day because I was a creative, and you can't tie down an artist and expect great work. Boy, was I wrong.

That mindset led to me never having a handle on my workload and having my business happen to me instead of me happening to my business. I was always putting out fires because I failed to plan, which led to planning to fail. No longer am I that person. I have finally understood that scheduling does, in fact, lead to the freedom to create. I am more creative now that I give myself time to create and it is not interrupted by something I failed to plan for.

Let's start with your calendar. Schedule everything. Everything includes things that have to do with your business and things that have to do with your personal life, your family, and your free time. One easy tool for how to ensure that all parts of your business get your attention every week is to dedicate days to certain aspects of the business.

For example:

- **Marketing Monday:** has everything to do with all the marketing required.
- **To-Do- List Tuesday:** use this day to run your errands and get all the little things done that take up a lot of time.
- **Website Wednesday:** use this time to ensure that all of your online offerings are up to date, that your website is up to date, LinkedIn listings, Google business listings, phone messages, automated systems with automated replies, etc.
- **Thoughtful Thursday:** use this day to review any education that you are enrolled in, commitments that you have made to create content, read books or articles that are invaluable to you and your business, and brainstorm what you need to do to take yourself to the next level.
- **Financial Friday:** use this day to review balance statements, profit-and-loss sheets, and bank accounts, pay bills, pay attention to accounts receivables, and ensure budgets are being managed.

Another great way to ensure that your time is being spent well is to use time-blocking in your calendar. Don't just say you will work on finances today. That is a broad commitment. Purposefully schedule into your calendar that you will spend 45 minutes reviewing budgets, 60 minutes reviewing accounts receivables and paying bills, 30 minutes updating dashboards, and another 60 minutes using the data received to create decisions for the next week, month, or year. By using this time-blocking method, you will ensure that the tasks get done with detail and to the level of satisfaction that will provide positive outcomes for your business.

Every Sunday, I sit down with my electronic calendar and my paper calendar. I transfer all of the concrete appointments into my days for the week and then look at the tasks that must get done and how long each one needs to be completed. Then I methodically assign each hour of my day to all of my commitments. All hours are scheduled and assigned to all the people I have commitments to – including myself!

When I schedule things for myself, it includes my workouts, meal prep, driving time for meetings, time driving the kids to their activities, reading books, and time with my partner. I schedule it all so I can make sure I have time for all the things that are important – most of all, me. If I am missing the mark at home, it throws my whole week off. If I miss looking after myself, it only takes a week or two for my body to remind me.

Essential Priorities

Think about what your essential priorities are. Many of us wear multiple hats in our lives. I am a mom, I am a performing arts studio owner, I am a business consultant and the CEO of a costume and dress code company, and I am also a private citizen. For each of the hats that I wear, I have three essential priorities.

Mom:

1. To raise my girls to be leaders and grow into their best selves
2. To teach them independent and critical thinking

3. To never let them see me sweat differences of opinion between their dad and me

Owner of a Performing Arts Studio:

1. To develop programs and systems that serve my company
2. To provide leadership and training to all of my staff
3. To create and execute all marketing and branding

Private Citizen:

1. Manage my household budget responsibly
2. Take care of my personal health
3. Prioritize relationships with my life partner, my family, and my friends

Knowing what these essential priorities are helps me to create systems in order to achieve success. You can take this to the next level by creating your essential priorities for your company. Take a look at all the different positions inside your company, and build out the essential functions for each position. An example of some positions at my performing arts school:

Program Director:

1. Classroom content and syllabus management
2. Program management
3. Staff communications

Office Manager:

1. Database and accounts management
2. Customer relations
3. Studio maintenance

Community Coordinator:

1. Community relationships and partnerships
2. Event management
3. Cross-promotion

Teacher:

1. Providing exceptional instruction: with age-appropriate content, developmentally appropriate content, music selections, and movement selections, and staying current with certifications and workshops
2. Creating dance community through motivation by attending studio events, completing student high-five cards and kindness-counts awards, nominating student of the month, and being a caring, alert, and available adult
3. Communicating through student retention, envisioning training pathways for students, with exams, competition, and performing opportunities, connecting with families for progress and concerns, creating report cards, and help with goal setting

Staff Touchpoints

If you aren't meeting regularly with your team, you don't have a team. What you have is a collection of boxes on an org chart.

Barbara Burke

How often do you meet with your team to ensure that they are all pointed in the right direction and moving toward the company mission and vision? I worked for years for a boss who

NEVER held a staff meeting – in over seven years! During the time I worked there, I had no connection to the other employees. I had no idea of the expectations of us as a team or an individual. In seven years, I never received a review of my performance or notes on how to be better. I had no feedback and no meetings. Needless to say, it was easy to leave when the time came because I did not have any connection to the mission or the people.

This happened to me at every job I held since high school until I started my own company. Such a simple thing that no one ensures happens regularly. When I began my own company, I knew I needed to provide a different experience than the one given to me. I quickly discovered that part-time employees are a lot harder to make mandatory meetings with. It is much harder to discipline people who only give a few hours a week to your company. They are also the ones who can do the most damage by not being informed. It made me rethink the idea of part-time employees and the roles they could hold in the company. While they are the least expensive in payroll, they are the most expensive to administer.

Keep regular communication touchpoints. Consider keeping regular meeting schedules. Look at the different departments in your company, and determine what type of meeting schedule best serves how fast decisions need to be made in each department.

- Who needs to be at each meeting?
- Do they require a daily huddle?
- Is a weekly meeting more acceptable?
- Is bi-weekly frequent enough?
- Do you need quarterly planning sessions?
- Do you need a weekly staff email?
- Do you need a staff Facebook page?
- Do you have an onboarding drip** of information for new employees?
- Do you train your staff how to treat your time and how to treat each other's time?
    - A text is urgent.

- A phone call needs to be returned as soon as possible.
- An email can be returned the next time you're in.
- Do you have a 24-hour rule? For example: sleep on it before you reply – especially if you are emotional.

**An onboarding drip refers to a series of emails that are automated to send on a predetermined schedule. Drips are extremely useful for repeatable processes that are predictable and helpful. They can help ensure that experiences for customers or staff are duplicated with the same level of excellence each time, regardless of when they enter the drip.

Sales & Marketing Tools and Systems

Do you have a stream of marketing that is consistently bringing you new leads or sales 24 hours a day, seven days a week? This has been a huge focus in my own business for the last five years, as new technology arises that allows us to sell at all hours of the day, making sales even while we are sleeping.

I was one of the first in my industry to implement online registration for dance lessons. Many owners were so concerned about what if someone registers into a level higher than they should, or for the wrong class, etc. All I could see was, what if you got new students? What if you could just connect with them later if the class is not the right one? Why create barriers for service if they want to buy from you? For over 19 years now, I have been working on ways to make it easier to do business with us. It turns out in those 19 years, the worries that owners had never became a problem, but we did enjoy great registration success year over year.

This is so important to stay on top of how to make things better. My mentor recently said: Amazon has ruined it for all of us. They have made every customer expect instant products or services, and most small businesses have so much work to do to meet those high consumer expectations.

All businesses need to have systems in place that are consistently bringing in new business and managing the current business, as well as reminding customers who have fallen off that you are still around doing business and you may still have a service or product they will need.

In my business, we have an information kit that you can download from our website. It collects names and email addresses, and emails the information automatically every time it is filled out. On the back end, my office gets a notification every time it is downloaded. They can then follow up with every inquiry. There are several ways to set these systems up and for different types of inquiries that allow you to funnel the inquiries based on content.

Look at your processes to determine if you are consistently bringing in new customers and serving current customers. Below are some questions to help you determine if you have some systems that need updating or implementing. You may also consider how easy it is doing business with you, and design service that tackles that challenge as well.

- Do you have documentation on lead generation and digital marketing engines?
- Have you documented how to use and update the website tools?
- Do you have help with artwork and graphic design?
- How will people connect with the other services you hire?
- What do you use as lead magnets and how often are they updated?
- How will you update your lead magnets?
- Do you have a customer newsletter?
- Who is responsible for writing it and gathering the content for your newsletter?
- Do you have an email management system to manage all the data and emails that come in through lead generation?
- Who manages the customer sales and the registration database?

- How do sales and registration get managed? And how often?
- Is there a handbook for staff?
- Is there a handbook for customers?
- Can handbooks be created as part of an onboarding drip?
- What are the communication platforms for both your team and your customers?
- Who is responsible for the team and customer communication platforms? During what times of the day?
- Do you have task-management or project-management software?
- Do you have a syllabus? Who is responsible for ensuring it is current? How often is it updated?
- Who is managing attendance?
- Who is responsible for the music or classroom content?
- Are you using cloud-based storage for your documents and other files?
- What calendar system are you using for staff and clients?
- Are you using cloud-based bookkeeping?
- Are you doing online banking?

Note, this list was initially published in *Insight*™ *Magazine* as – Building A Dream Team: How to Restructure Your Staff.

Putting It All Together:

The way to get started is to quit talking and begin doing.

Walt Disney

Now that we have discussed some of the systems that we really need to get to work on, we need to talk about what to do with all the information. Where do we store it? How do we reference it readily and easily? We start by getting it all down in one place.

Documentation

Action is the only way to make progress. Take action now; don't wait for a convenient time. It can't be overemphasized.

Mike Michalowicz

There are two types of documentation required inside a small business:
1. How to do something
2. When to do something

When I started out, I had no idea what systems needed to be built. I would create things as they became apparent. In the beginning, I was doing almost all the tasks, so the knowledge lived in my head. I eventually hired help, but I had no way to train them and we did not document things as we went, leading to further issues down the line when that person was no longer with the company. This is especially frustrating if someone who has been with you a long time takes an extreme amount of knowledge with them. You miss tasks they used to do, and you only discover them after the situation has become urgent. **Don't let this happen to you! It is entirely preventable!**

I spent many years reacting to my business. Because nothing was documented, my business was always happening to me. This type of operation style is exhausting and completely unnecessary if you take action starting now. Now I spend my mornings being proactive, getting ahead of tasks and projects, and my afternoon is spent reacting to client and staff needs. I am no longer worried that I have forgotten something that will be catastrophic – like payroll. I know that everything is getting done at the right time and with the correct attention to detail. **My business no longer runs me – I run my business.**

Many micro-businesses and small businesses do not have sufficient documentation of all of their processes and systems. This includes small things such as opening and closing procedures, balancing a cash register, and how to clean machinery or the facility. You can also include more detailed things, such as how to run monthly payments, how to order for inventory, and more. Do you have a place where your staff can locate the 'how to' and 'when to' of your company?

Check out the Action Items at the end of this chapter to kickstart getting your systems documented and up to speed for your growth.

Action Item – Job Descriptions

Redefine Job Descriptions:
1. *Write out all the tasks to be done in the whole organization, one task per card.*
2. *Lay them all out on a large table or large flooring space.*
3. *Everyone on the team picks up the ones they are doing.*
4. *Use the cards picked up to create each job description.*
5. *Evaluate remaining tasks for assignment to existing staff or hire.*

Redistribute Job Descriptions:
1. *Write out all the tasks to be done in the whole organization, one task per card.*
2. *Lay them all out on a large table or floor space.*
3. *Everyone on the team picks up the ones they are doing.*
4. *Take note of which cards are left over.*
5. *Ask people to categorize which tasks they are doing, which ones they are not good at, and which ones they do not want to do.*
6. *Ask people to pick up tasks they would prefer to be doing.*
7. *Use the cards picked up to create each job description.*
8. *Evaluate remaining tasks for assignment to existing staff or hire.*

Action Item – Attributes Activity

Look at what roles are available in your organization with regard to sales, service, and support. What are 10 attributes required for your dream team players in each area?

One of the great things about being an entrepreneur in the arts is that we are constantly choreographing our businesses too, not just for stage. Here is a teaching from Misty Lown blended with Darren Hardy's High-Performance Forum about attributes required for each construct.

Sales	Service	Support
Who is in this role: 1. 2. 3.	Who is in this role: 1. 2. 3.	Who is in this role: 1. 2. 3.
What attributes do they need: 1. 2. 3. 4. 5. 6. 7. 8. 9. 10.	What attributes do they need: 1. 2. 3. 4. 5. 6. 7. 8. 9. 10.	What attributes do they need: 1. 2. 3. 4. 5. 6. 7. 8. 9. 10.

Action Item – Documentation

1. Commit to recording one process per week.
2. Include several employees in writing up one process per week.
3. Record all the steps involved.
4. Use a template, ensuring all processes are recorded in the same format.
5. Ask another employee to do the task using the steps provided.
6. Edit the steps with the feedback from the employee.
7. Determine where all these processes will be recorded for access by all employees.
8. Record the date of the process and the name of the person who recorded it; in the future it can be determined if it is still current.

Many of the tasks done in your business are repetitive, either hourly, daily, weekly, monthly, or annually. By creating a process that helps you to repeat these tasks at the right intervals, you can free up your mental load for more creativity and growth in your business, rather than jumping from fire to fire.

Take the time to record many of the items that repeat in your business. Open up your calendar and make a list of the things that have happened in your business over the last month that will repeat in the future. Another option is to list all your tasks for four weeks to get a start on the list of systems that need to be recorded.

- *Opening and closing*
- *Deposits to the bank*
- *Writing cheques for payments*
- *Payroll*
- *Ordering products*
- *Answering emails*
- *Cleaning the facility*
- *Marketing tasks*
- *Scheduling staff*
- *Updating budgets*
- *Seasonal decoration*
  **The list goes on

Once you have recorded a large list of tasks that are repetitive in nature, start to group them into categories. This can be done in categories by department or by frequency. You will also want to consider who the project or task is assigned to. This way, if someone goes on extended leave or no longer works for your company, projects and tasks that they were responsible for will not fall through the cracks. Determine where this information will be stored in a way that it can be updated and accessible.

CHAPTER 7 – FINANCES 2.0

You've got to tell your money what to do or it will leave.

Dave Ramsey

I am coming back to finances because over my years of education and fixing the wrong in my business and in my clients' businesses, it always comes back to finances. Without fail, it is always a lack of understanding of how everything works together that causes the mess. By not understanding every single piece of the puzzle and how they are intertwined, there is always room for mistakes, and sometimes they can be enormous. In fact, very successful programs can hide the failures of others simply because we do not have enough detail to see where the holes are.

I coached one of my clients through a terrible financial mess. Michelle was running a family business that had 50 years under its belt. She was running it with the same tuition model her mother and grandmother had used, because that was the way it had always been done—no other reason. She hadn't raised prices in years, even though she had huge increases in operating costs. To start with, she had to peel back the layers of all the sources of revenue and all the expenses to understand where the leak was. Where was all the money going? We discovered that she had several programs where she was not making money; in fact, she was paying to provide them! Using the steps in this chapter, I am going to show you how we found where the exact issues were and how we managed to fix them.

In the previous chapter on finances, we discussed the basic information that one requires to make good business decisions.

We discussed understanding how your accounting program works and hiring someone who can do this for you if this is not your expertise. Taking your finances to the next level requires a piece of deeper knowledge.

The first place to dive in is pricing the product or service that we are selling. Earlier, we talked about pricing items similarly to competitors in the market out of ignorance of expenses that we don't yet know about. That happens because we have no idea what we need to price products or services until we have a real idea of the actual expenses. Once we have a better idea of the actual cost to provide the service or product because we have been in business for a while and now have some real data to work with, we can go back and revisit that pricing structure.

Now we know what type of staffing needs are required and how their skill set is compensated. We also know how much it costs to deliver the product, and understand how much it costs to run our brick-and-mortar space. Now go back and plug those numbers in to find out what is the real product or service cost. If we are in a service-based industry and the person delivering the service has a different wage than another employee delivering a similar service, we will need to have a spreadsheet that helps determine the cost per person. This is why we might see in some models a senior specialist who charges more than an entry-level service provider. Their expertise and experience in the industry are being compensated through the price that they charge for their service. We need to ensure that our products and services are also being priced in such a manner as to take into account the variety of compensation packages in our team.

Where to start on this daunting task? One step at a time:

1. Budget
2. Burn rate
3. Projections
4. Proformas
5. Pricing structure
6. Dashboards

Budget

> *Don't tell me what you value. Show me*
> *your budget, and I'll tell you what you*
> *value.*
>
> *Joe Biden*

This process needs to be set annually, and depending on how often the company has transactions, it may need to be visited either weekly, monthly, or at another frequency that makes sense. Using last year's data and the chart of accounts inside our bookkeeping software, we will be able to set up a new budget for the current year, based on the growth rate anticipated. If we are anticipating a 5% growth, then we can make some assumptions that we will see a 5% increase in sales and some associated increases in expenses to deliver those sales. By extension, if we anticipate a contraction in the company, we can predict a loss by percentage and the associated expenses with a loss in sales.

The main point is that once we have a season or two of books, we will be much better able to create budgets that make sense, including all of the right categories that are useful to us. They will take into account any cycles the business goes through, and we will be able to budget according to those cycles. As mentioned earlier in the book, this is something to visit on Financial Friday to ensure that the company is creating revenue and expenses in line with what our predictions are. This will prevent any surprises at year-end that were unable to stay inside of the predictions we've made. We will be able to course-correct throughout the fiscal year to ensure we reach the company's goals and to stay inside of the budget we created.

In Michelle's case, she had no budget and 50 years' worth of books. So we started with last year's numbers to create this year's budget. She set to work understanding all the revenue categories and all the expense categories. Along the way, she was able to provide some instruction to her accountant about ways to improve how the books were set up so that she could make better use of the information in the future. She made changes to the names of the revenue categories and expense categories and what went into each one, so she would be better able to make use of the information collected in the future.

Burn Rate

This term refers to the cost of having the doors open for an hour. How much money does it cost to open the doors to potentially sell the service or the product? This helps determine a base rate for the service or product. We need to get away from "We're just glad to have a sale," and move to a place where we have to make sure that the sale matches the output to make that sale happen.

Gather up all of the expense items that are a result of running the business, such as rent, utilities, marketing, etc. (include admin employees, exclude any employees required to deliver the product), and divide against the number of hours the business is open. This number tells us the minimum number of sales needed to open the front door before hiring an employee to deliver the service.

Expenses/number of hours open = Burn Rate
$100,000 / 2000 hours (40 hours per week, 50 weeks per year)
= $50 per hour
This means that every time the door opens, $50 per hour is the minimum I need to cover before a service is provided.

The next thing we need to determine is how many products or services you can deliver per hour. For example, in a dance class, you might be able to sell up to 10 students in the same time slot and deliver a group class. Now you are going to use the burn rate to figure out the minimum number of students needed in a classroom to make a class viable. Alternatively, if you are selling something as a private lesson or an individual product, the minimum you need to reach is one product or service. You will need to make sure that you cover the burn rate as well as the wages of the person delivering.

$50 /month x 10 students = $500 / four weeks per month = $125 per hour
$50 /month x four students = $200 / four weeks per month = $50 per hour

In this example, you have to enroll a minimum of four students per hour to cover expenses such as rent, insurance, etc. But the instructor wage is still not in there – you need to enroll more than four students or else increase the rates at which you sell the product. This exercise helps you to see if your rates are accurately set for the wages you pay the teacher to deliver the service. You can see that our calculations are slowly working us into correcting our pricing.

When Michelle did this exercise, the first thing that jumped out at her was that she always thought she needed four students in a class to break even. It turns out it was actually six. Now that was valuable information.

Projections

A budget tells us what we can't afford, but it doesn't keep us from buying it.

William Feather

Another tool that can be used to help determine pricing and potential revenue are projections. We can create a spreadsheet where every single product or time slot is listed, along with the associated current revenue, potential revenue, current expenses, potential expenses, and the amount of money left on the table when we do not sell out of that time slot or product.

Service Timeslot	# sold	Max #	Current income	Current Expenses	Max Revenue	Difference	Current Revenue	Revenue Unrealized
Mon 5:00 pm	4	12	4*50= $200	$25/hr Instructor	12*50 = $600	$400	$200 - 25 = $175	$375
Tue 6:00 pm	7	18	7*50 = $350	$30/hr Instructor	18*50 = $900	$550	$350-$30 = $320	$490
Fri 5:30 pm	20	20	20*50= $1000	$60 /hr 2x Instructor	20*50= $1000	$0	$1000-60 = $940	$0

This is an extremely useful tool in deciding how much money to spend on marketing, whether adding another instructor to a classroom is an appropriate choice, and how much more revenue you have the potential of bringing in.

Remember Michelle? My client with the family-run studio with 50 years of history and no price increases recently? We did this exercise. The results were powerful. She discovered that she had some instructors that were being paid higher rates than the classes were generating in revenue. She was able to pinpoint which classes were losing money. She was shocked to discover that she was paying for those teachers to have a job rather than the teachers creating enough revenue to pay for themselves and generate profit for the business.

Proformas

Proformas are a great tool for making three- and five-year predictions in the growth of the company. Many lenders will ask for these types of documents and calculations when considering whether to loan the company funds for growth. Lenders want to see there are numbers on what growth looks like inside the business. By completing the above activities on projections for a current year, we can use those numbers to create three- and five-year projections of growth. Combine that with the company's typical growth percentages and we can start to create some powerful visuals of the company's potential.

Proformas can be easily created using the budgeting tool in accounting programs.

1.   Export the last three years actuals to a spreadsheet.
2.   Add the budget to the same spreadsheet.

3. Make several columns for three to five years of projections.
4. Include growth projections for expansion, new equipment, and future plans for the business.
5. Include best-case, worst–case, and probable scenario predictions for each year.

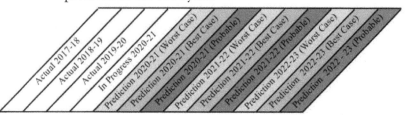

Once Michelle started to see the proformas shaping up, she was able to see how she could start putting into the plan her desire to move into a larger location. She had an idea of what she needed for buildout and cash reserve. She could create scenarios based on good, bad and average years of business and start to see how she could make her goal of a new location come to life.

Pricing Structure

Now that we have created some of the numbers that we need to have at the ready, we can look at pricing the product correctly. As mentioned before, there are three levers we can pull to increase revenue. Building a spreadsheet to play with these is a great tool. The three levers we can pull are:

1. The number of customers: Student number
2. The amount each sale is worth: Base
3. The number of sales per customer: Units

Base	#of Students	Base tuition	units	Monthly total	Monthly Increase	Annual Increase
0%	600	$50	1	$30,000	$ -	$300,000
0%	672	$50	2.2	$73,920	$43,920	$739,200
5%	600	$53	1	$31,500	$ 1,500	$315,000
5%	672	$53	2.2	$77,616	$47,616	$776,160
10%	600	$55	1	$33,000	$ 3,000	$330,000
10%	672	$55	2.2	$81,312	$51,312	$813,120
15%	600	$58	1	$34,500	$ 4,500	$345,000
15%	672	$58	2.2	$85,008	$55,008	$850,080

* 30 Min Classes, $50 per month

In Michelle's case, she knew she needed to increase her rates in order to cover the wages and earnings needed for her relocation goal. By using this tool, she was able to see a five-year plan for tuition rates, number of students, and number of units required to reach her goals. She was then able to plan what that rollout could look like to her clients and strategize the best times for those increases.

Dashboards

Dashboards are another fantastic tool to give us a current snapshot of what the company is doing at any given moment. The magic lies in understanding which metrics are appropriate to measure more frequently than others. As we start to build a dashboard, here are some metrics to consider, including:

- Number of leads in every day
- Number of leads converted into actual purchases
- Total sales number for the day
- Any lost sales or refunds
- Accounts receivable
- Accounts payable

- Amount of money owed in the next 30 days, and who it is owed to
- Amount of money to be received in the next 30 days, and who it is coming from
- Amount of money in the bank
- Amount of money owed in loans, credit cards, and other debt

The idea is that the dashboard should be able to give accurate information that will allow instant, educated decisions. Can we spend that money on marketing? Are we able to jump on that opportunity because there is enough cash on hand? Can we expand the product line, services, or even location? Are we able to make a big spend on new equipment?

Below is an example of a basic dashboard. Depending on the metrics that we wish to measure, you will discover better ways for the business numbers to be tracked. Start with a spreadsheet, and start listing the metrics that indicate the health of the business. Determine what the targets would look like for the growth that we are aiming for in our goals. Then set up simple formulas to help determine how close we are or if we are succeeding.

Dashboards are so essential to monitoring KRA in a business that I dedicated a full day of training in MTJGD™ Systems Masters Day in a deep dive to understand how they interact with our business goals. Here is a basic version, however as you use them, your system will come to measure many facets of your business beyond the basic format suggested here:

	ACTUAL	TARGET	% to GOAL
Leads			
Trial Classes Booked			
Full Season Enrolled			
Sessional			
Customer Touch Points			
AR			
Payments owed			

This only works if it is kept updated on a regular basis. Determine who on your team is responsible for updating which metrics. We also need to determine how often this gets updated. Is it daily, weekly, or biweekly? What checkpoint makes the most sense for your business and the volume coming through?

You may discover after working with these for a while that you have several categories and your dashboard gets a bit more detailed. This is a good thing. The more pieces we measure, the more it will change. If there is a change to make in the business or a special marketing campaign that needs tracking, add it to the dashboard, where we can measure the results.

Watching the numbers change over time for a goal you have set allows the team to really see results and change. It can be inspiring and may cause your employees to ask for other items to be measured too, such as outstanding tasks or long-term goals for departments. Over time, you will start to make the dashboard unique to your company, and it will become the tool that you can go back to every day for the decisions you need to make.

For Michelle, the dashboard became her business brain. She used it every day to make decisions. Did she have the resources for a guest teacher, could she afford a new printer, was there enough work to hire another staff person? Once she understood which metrics she needed to measure, and what success was for her business, she was able to collect data regularly and use it to make decisions. She no longer looked at the bank account and hoped she was making a good decision.

Action Item – Budgets

Go now and look at your software for accounting, or speak to your bookkeeper/accountant to discuss how you can easily set this up and pull the reports whenever you need them.

Action Item – Burn Rate

Find all the numbers you need to make this calculation before moving on to the next step.
    Expenses/ number of hours open = Burn Rate
    $100,000 / 2000 hours (40 hours per week, 50 weeks per year) = $50 per hour.

Action Item – Projections

Take the time to create the projection chart to understand the impact on one of the services, departments or products you provide. Be sure to calculate the minimum and maximums alongside the current revenues and expenses. Be sure to note how much money is left on the table when you do not maximize the operations in that department.

Action Item – Proforma

Create a proforma and begin using it to make your decisions on when to afford new staff, equipment, or expansion activities.

Action Item – Pricing Structure

Create a chart around the three levers. Then start playing with each lever and what would happen with 5%, 10%, and 15% increases. Then create a plan for how you will use this tool over the next three to five years of business increases.

Action Item – Dashboards

Start with a spreadsheet and start listing the metrics that indicate the health of the business. Determine what the targets would look like for the goals. Then set up simple formulas to help determine how close you are or if you are succeeding.

CHAPTER 8 – SUPPORT SYSTEMS

*Surround yourself with only people who
are going to lift you higher.*

Oprah Winfrey

When my business was running on hopes and dreams instead of data and knowledge, it was a beast. It had taken on a life of its own. It haunted me every hour of every day. Without setting up support systems inside my business, I was always standing in a field of landmines, waiting for the next explosion.

Too many students, not enough structure, too many staff, not enough leadership, not enough patriots to help carry the mission, too many mercenaries working on their own glory. I could not see this for what it was at the time. All I knew was there was always another complaint or problem at work and no relief, ever.

My support at home was running thin. I had no personal skills to shut work off. I had no work network to help me problem-solve and so I continued to swirl the drain. My mental health struggled, and my marriage became strained. I began to lose hope. My business became everything – it was all I could think about – eat, sleep, talk about. The people closest to me became tired of my conversation topics, always around an angry parent or a staff person who needed to be corrected. This is where every trap you can fall into was strapped like dynamite to my heart and to my business.

I was in a position where I defined myself as a Dance Studio Owner and in no other way.

In order to remove the dynamite wrapped around my heart, I had to become more self-sufficient and find an identity that was not attached to my business. This was when I started to look outside of my small circle for help. I started to look for books to help me be more efficient, to improve my leadership skills, to interview better so I could make better hires. To improve my systems so they didn't leave me wondering what I had missed and how it would show up. I found more than books: I found podcasts, online courses, in-person courses, and the jackpot – industry associations that had a focus on better practices.

Different conferences, networks, education opportunities, mentors, and coaches are available in almost every industry. Finding the best ones takes work and connections. Mastermind groups and how to use them is also a skill that has to be developed. Growing the muscle of how to keep your work at work and turn it off at the end of the day has to be exercised to become skilled at it. Knowing when to level up in education and support is key for development professionally and personally.

I began building my support systems by remembering where I came from. I came from education. When I was growing up, I loved to read and learn and see things working in action. Somewhere along the way, I got sucked into having to know all the answers and was no longer seeking them. It's the wrong attitude. Experts are always learning, reading, and discovering. They never stop. It's what makes them experts. Somehow in the busy of "being a business owner," I stopped learning and got caught in the busy of owning. The cycle of knowledge and action became broken and became just reaction. It was time to get back to a healthier process.

Books

You cannot open a book without learning something.

Confucius

The world of books is never disappointing. A mentor of mine once said that the world's most successful CEOs read upwards of 50 books a year. I found a statistic that the equivalent of a bachelor's degree is 58 books. Imagine getting a business bachelor's degree almost every year you are in business. Learning should never stop. Looking back on myself before this discovery, I realized I had stopped reading. Completely. I used to love reading fiction and non-fiction, but it had been years since I had added to my education. I felt I did not have time.

Enter the AUDIOBOOK.

This is an amazing tool! Now I didn't have to make time to turn pages or bring the "work" book into the bedroom at night – I was able to "read" any time. I made a rule: – the car did not run without a book playing, I could make dinner to it, get ready in the morning to it – all of a sudden, I had all this extra knowledge available to me, and I was able to do it without much change to my schedule. I love this "extra education time" that I was able to add to my day.

With this new "opportunity" for education in my life, I was ready to start seeing what else was out there. I started to make notes of books that authors would refer to and add them to my list. I began to ferociously consume content. I would go to the library and take out audiobooks from anyone that I could find at the time: Jim Rohn, Brian Tracey, Sean Covey, Timothy Ferris, Jim Collins, Jack Welch, etc. Today I still manage to get through several podcasts and a book every two weeks. – It is so important to keep flushing your mind with new ideas and thoughts to help you push forward in continued growth.

Conferences

The capacity to learn is a gift; the ability to learn is a skill; the willingness to learn is a choice.

Brian Herbert

Not all conferences are created equal. I have been to my fair share of industry conferences in my field, and there are so many approaches. You really do need to find one that fits your strategies and needs for growth. These conferences can turn into networking groups and relationships that stand the test of time.

I believe the right thing presents itself as you need it. The first few conferences I attended focused on the feel-good aspect of our businesses—that we are an admirable industry for how we grow children and had a focus on best practices for the children. It helped me lay the beginning foundation for our culture in our company and what made us different from our local competitors. At some point, I started to feel that I needed more to grow to the next level. I realized I needed to learn more about the time wealth of a business. I didn't want to work 60 to 70 hours a week with no end in sight. I needed to learn more about working harder on the business, not in it, for longevity's sake.

Around that time, an invitation to a new conference that I did not know about came in the mail. I decided to attend. After all, it had a money-back guarantee, so there was not much to lose. I was blown away by the systems that I needed in place but was unaware of. So much knowledge in the room, so many successful people to learn from and create relationships with. As Lorne Michaels' has been attributed as saying, "Never be the smartest person in the room." I had my eyes opened wide at this event and continued attending for several years before feeling like I was getting better at tackling the systems and strategies being presented. I had also made some great relationships that allowed me to start getting things solved at work rather than taking things home. I have a network of resources, people who had been where I was and were able to help lead me to solutions in a healthy way. I was able to start leaving work at work. It was so freeing!

I found a third networking group, which is still my networking group today. This group had the perfect blend of culture and business acuity that I was seeking. I could easily see what needed to be worked on, where I needed to seek education to master my challenges. I deepened my relationships with successful business owners and soon found myself working hard to run alongside them. I was motivated by their success and that I could have that too.

Over the years, I have learned how to conference smarter, which I will share. When you attend these events, you receive so much information. You can form so many wonderful intentions and see the blue sky and opportunities that could be created for yourself and your business. Yet, for some reason, many people never manage to do much with what they learn. I was determined not to let that be me. I had to learn the best way to activate my learning and ideas, as well as ensure my team did not get overwhelmed by my desire to implement, every time I arrived home from a conference. I didn't want them to dread my ongoing education and to fear the outcomes.

I used to take a fresh notebook to each event – I discovered that it was too easy to shove the notebook and the conference binder onto the shelf after a couple of weeks and never crack it open again. Then I learned this fact studied by German Psychologist Hermann Ebbinghaus called "The Forgetting Curve":

You forget 50% of what you have just learned within one hour of learning it.
You forget 70% of what you learned within one day of learning it.
You forget 90% of what you learned within one week of learning it.

If this is true, I had to find a better way to ensure my knowledge didn't get forgotten and my time wasted – after all, it costs a lot of my own company's hard-earned money to send me to these events. I needed to ensure that I got my value. I needed to make sure the most work could be captured within that first week.

Today I use a system at events. I always begin preparation at least two weeks before the event. I clear my inbox, finish any large projects that need wrapping up, ensure everything is prepped for my absence – even making sure everything is covered at home.

The meals, the pets, the driving to activities – it all has to be taken care of so that I can focus and get the most out of the time I spend away from my regular life. I start to think about what the three biggest questions are that I need to answer or problems I need to solve. This will help shape my conversations and the time I spend chatting with people at the event. The last thing I do is put an email responder on that highlights that I am away learning and that, to prevent overload upon my return, emails will be deleted. If it is important, please resend when I return.

I travel to the event a day early so I can continue to clear my mind and not be rushing from the airport with delays that are inevitable, etc. I want to ensure I am fully present. I make sure I have a good night's rest, so I am ready for a heavy day of learning and dreaming of possibilities. Make sure you have everything you need: computers, chargers, notepads, name tags, water bottles, meal plans, etc. Get it all in place so you can get the most out of this amazing opportunity.

I have developed a note-system strategy for during the event. Every idea or thought I have gets its own card, page number, and topics added for reference if I need to go back. I have multiple companies now, so ideas that get sparked get a company name on the card as well. Topics are colour-coded:

- Green – Finance
- Blue – Systems
- Pink – Staffing
- Yellow – Next Season/Fiscal Year
- White – Anything Else

This allows me to sort my cards at the end of the event – which also has a system.

At the end of the event, I always plan to stay an extra day. This time has been so valuable to me. Often, we leave a conference, we rush to get back home to the kids and the business, and we get sucked back into the whirlwind. We become part of the 80% who forget they were ever even at the event. This extra day is a brilliant use of time. I use the evening when the conference ends to lay out every single card on the bed or floor of my room. I start to make piles for each business, then business by business, I go through this process:

- Ideas or cards that will take five min or less to execute
- Ideas or cards that will take 10-15 min or less
- Cards that refer to books, podcasts, or other educational material to seek out
- What is left gets sorted into priority:
  - Impact on the bottom line – takes time
  - Impact on the bottom line – short time investment
  - Less impact on the bottom line – takes time
  - Less impact on the bottom line – short time investment

These piles of cards now help me decide which cards are the most important to implement the fastest, based on the business needs at hand. Then I start to calendar a strategy for when we will work on the ideas and cards. This means that when I get home, I will be sure to implement and continue to improve my business in the days following an event.

Now I can often get through this part of the process on the evening the event is finished. However, here is the real magic of my system. I spend the next whole day working through the pile of cards! I work through the five-min pile and then through the 10–15-min pile for every company. Before noon, I have implemented so much content and made so much progress. It is so rewarding and astonishing! Then I get to work on the next card that I determined is most important. What is significant about this is the volume of work that gets done because I am off-site, I am not being bothered, and people know I am still away. The amazingness that comes from a full workday after a few days of inspiration has been something you cannot put a price tag on. I know that after every conference I am getting so much value from being there and implementing immediately.

What to do with all those index cards? As I complete each one, I put a tear almost all the way through, and I keep that stack of completed cards and tasks. I have a rubber band around them, and every time I add to it, I am reminded of the progress I have made. I need to build in the tiny celebrations because I am often on to the next thing. Celebrate that I have not forgotten that I was at the event and that I have moved the needle on my business and gotten my value from the training and time away to focus on the business instead of being in the business.

There you have it! My conference secret sauce!

Networking

> *If you want to go fast, go alone. If you want to go far, go with others.*
>
> *African Proverb*

Networking used to terrify me. How could I circulate in a room of successful people? I had a business that was hanging by a thread, low self-esteem, and the belief that had been confirmed over and over again that I was "just a dance teacher." So many times at dinner parties I would say I own a dance studio and be met with:

"Oh, that's nice. What else do you do?"

"Nothing else, thank you. This is my full-time job."

I am running a dance school the size of a large elementary school. No one ever asks a principal of an elementary school what else they do. The job is enough all on its own. Just because it is your hobby doesn't mean you can't make a living at it. But at the time they were right, because I was not making a living at it. I needed to become better in every aspect. I had to work really hard on my self-esteem and confidence. I needed to stand strong in my career choice and own my place in the room. This is where education helps. I was so absorbed in my business that I had forgotten the skill of listening. You don't always have to be the one talking. In fact, people love to talk about their own successes, and you can learn much more from listening than you can from talking.

This has been a huge help for me in a networking space. You really only need a few questions in your pocket and then some really amazing listening ears. If you can help someone else tell you more about what they do and how they do it, you are always sure to learn something. Listen for understanding, too—be ready with some questions to show you are paying attention and to find out the little nuggets that you can learn from.

By reading a few great books like *The Art of Conversation* by Catherine Blyth or *How to Win Friends and Influence People* by Dale Carnegie, and so many more, you will learn that what you really need are a few great questions in your repertoire and the ability to really listen when people speak. This came as wonderful news to an ambivert like me. I love a stage to perform and present on, but I do not love small conversations. I find them challenging and a true skill that I have to constantly work on. By understanding how to navigate the room and to really listen and ask great questions, I have learned so much more than I used to at these types of events.

Now let's dive into formalized networking groups. You may have been approached by a networking group where you have a fee to participate, perhaps there are levels to that fee, and you are skeptical of why one level would be better than another and if it is worth the money. I was skeptical too, and I am here to say, you get what you pay for. If you are dabbling at a basic level or introductory level, you will get far less than if you jump all the way in. I spent several years on the fringe of a group, thinking, "I can't afford to go all-in." Is this even a smart use of my money? When you are at that lower level, you will meet the less successful owners and more skeptics. The more successful people already know that the best nuggets and information are at the highest level.

Then meeting the less successful people started to confirm that it might not be the best spend. Those are the people that say it can't be done. It costs too much. I don't know how to do it, etc. I told myself, after yet another conference of sitting at a table with a bunch of people who were so negative, that I just couldn't do it anymore. I was ready to quit. I filled in my feedback for the event, and they called me. Without that call, I would not be where I am today. They said, "Try one year of the upper level. If you still feel the value is not there, then we will refund you the difference if you had stayed at the basic level."

People! I am here to tell you: you get what you pay for. One year of sitting at the big kid's table was all I needed to pull up my bootstraps and move the needle on my business. By not being the smartest person at the table, I learned so much. I created some amazing relationships that have become dear friends around the world. I have contacts that run all kinds of businesses, and I can learn from each type. I learned there is a right and a wrong way to network. I am just sad that it took me so long to find the right table for me.

Jim Rohn famously said that we are the average of the five people we spend the most time with. If your five people are not making your average higher, you need to find five better people. This is so true in networking. Networking is a skill and a tool that can fast-track your results. You need to hone it and use it well. Don't forget to really look at the five people you hang out with. This is true all the time. Are your best friends helping you get better? Do they maintain the status quo? Or are they sliding backwards and taking you with them? If your friends, family, and co-workers are not as driven as you, eventually, you will stay where they are. If they challenge you to be better, then you will grow. We are what we surround ourselves with.

Business Coaches

> *Everyone needs a coach. It doesn't matter whether you're a basketball player, a tennis player, a gymnast, or a bridge player.*
>
> *Bill Gates*

I had never given much thought to the idea of a business coach in my early years of ownership. It is silly. We learn that if you join a sports team, you will have a coach. The coach is there to help you learn the rules and the skills you need to help yourself and the team. Then somehow after we finish our formal education, are we just supposed to go through life without any more coaches? That makes no sense.

This light bulb went on for me slowly. I had joined a networking group that I loved. I was learning so much and was becoming so much more resilient in my knowledge and business acumen, but I was not seeing what was in front of me. I was in this relationship for two years before I was able to see that I was actually in a relationship with a business coach. Then I started to make all kinds of connections. When we want better physical fitness, we hire personal training coaches; when we want healthier nutrition, we hire nutrition coaches. Once I started to connect all these ideas, I was able to look at New Year's resolutions so much differently. The reason I was not getting those big goals is because I was not hiring a coach to get there. I needed the accountability and the pathway to be drawn for me. I am not meant to know all the answers; just be humble enough and clever enough to ask for help and to get it from the best places.

Want to be better at Facebook ads? Get a Facebook coach. Want to be better at finances? Get a financial coach. If the finances are huge and never going away, that coach may become an important and permanent part of your success team. We have health teams: family doctors, naturopaths, massage therapists, and chiropractors, etc. Why not have a business success team too? One that comprises your business coach, your accountant, your marketing coach, and everyone else that you need to be successful? We are not meant to be experts in every field. There is always someone who can shorten the distance for you to get from A to B. Be sure to seek out those people and solutions – your success actually depends on it. There is a coach for EVERYTHING.

Mentors

---

*A mentor is someone who allows you to
see the hope inside yourself.*

Oprah Winfrey

Mentors are not the same as business coaches. Mentors are those who have travelled the path before you, likely in another industry. They offer sage wisdom and loving nudges for growth. They tend to be long-term relationships that grow in depth over time. Coaches tend to be for a shorter period of time, enough time to learn the skills and start to see results. Coaches tend to be specific about the skills that they train. Mentors tend to have no formal training to be a mentor, just a desire to share their learning and expertise with another person to improve their successful experiences.

Why is finding a mentor so important? A mentor has been there before you. They can offer advice and be a sounding board at critical times in your career. They often offer hard-to-find advice and key understandings to help shape important decisions. They can often make introductions to important people you may need to know and open doors that, without them, may not have been possible. They offer career guidance from experience and learning.

Finding a mentor is so important to the longevity of great success. It is also challenging to find a mentor if you feel you don't have one already. The best relationships have a natural match to them. They are not forced. Here are a few suggestions for where to get started:

1. Look for networking events.
2. Attend entrepreneur hotspots.
3. Look inside your professional circle – former bosses or coaches.
4. Family friends.
5. Small business development centres.

What to ask a mentor when you find one? This is a delicate process. These relationships take time and are built on trust and mutual respect for one another. Take the time to find out more about their journey. Be ready to listen and ask if it is okay to take notes. Think about questions to ask that are thoughtful. Share a bit about yourself and your goals. Always leave time and space for them to share their wisdom along the way. Mentors are one of life's greatest gifts. They have so much to share and help us understand. Always share your gratitude with your mentor. They are a treasure.

Productivity

> *Focus on being productive instead of busy.*
>
> *Tim Ferriss*

With all of the previous ideas in mind, we should talk about productivity and what it really means. I used to believe I was amazing at productivity. I used to proudly speak of my flawless multitasking skills and ability to do many things with great speed and accuracy every shift. People would ask me, "How are you today?" I would reply with, "Busy, so very busy." And I was "busy." Now with more knowledge about productivity, I actually despise the word "busy."

Busy means low productivity. Busy means a lot of activity with little result. Busy is what happens to your time if you do not get clear about how you want to spend it. Now when people ask me, "How was your day?" I get excited to answer with "Productive." Productive means I can define what got done and how well. It feels like a list got checked off, or big projects were tackled and completed. Productive does not have wasted time, unfinished business, or missed tasks. Let's talk about what makes a day productive.

What is productivity? What do we know about it? Why is it such a big deal in the workplace? Many people think that productivity looks like:

- Alone with no distractions
- A bright, clean workspace
- Having all your drinks lined up
- Snacks within arm's reach
- Oil blend for focus
- Getting distracting tasks done, like tidying the kitchen, etc.
- Being ready to work: showing up as your best self, on time, ready to work
- Having all your supplies ready: pen, notebooks, highlighters, etc.

And who wouldn't be productive if you had all those items lined up and ready to help you get to work? But are all these items really productive?

These ideas are actually more about surroundings and environment. We might need some of these items to get closer to productivity, but they are not really what productivity is made of... so what is it really?

Productivity is about focus and having information readily available in a manner that is easy to consume. Let's talk about how to prepare for great feats of accomplishment!

Gathering Places

Without clearly defined gathering points for this stuff, you lose time, money and tax forms. That can't be good for business!

Dave Crenshaw

How many places in your life do you have things accumulating?

- Your purse/wallet
- Your car console
- Counter in your kitchen
- Dreaded junk drawer
- Pile of papers in your office
- Pile of papers in your room
- Work bag

What about emails and messages?

- Personal phone
- Work phone
- Personal email
- Work email
- Facebook
- Instagram
- Messenger

I am sure if you think hard, you may even come up with more than this. According to Dave Crenshaw, the average person has over 26 gathering places where they accumulate information that needs to be processed. How on earth are you supposed to be productive if you need to go to 26 places to find everything you have to get done?

Get out a notepad and work through every place you have information. Use the items above to help you get all those places noted. Now that you have your exhaustive list, are you similar to the average of 26 places? Did it surprise you where you keep all the information you need to get through a day?

What if I told you that in *How to Tame Your Office*, Dave Crenshaw also recommends that you only have six places!? The most productive people have found a way to narrow down all those places into these six key locations:

1. Physical Inbox
2. Portable inbox – travels with you
3. Email inbox – just one
4. Voicemail – just one
5. Note pad – paper or digital
6. Wild card – if what you need is not mentioned

Could you imagine a world where you only had to go to six places to gather the information you needed to get on with your tasks?

Squirrel syndrome is a term we use inside our business. Squirrel syndrome is another problem to contend with. Squirrel syndrome is having your eye caught by every shiny object that comes along. It is endless distractions that add up to so many wasted hours in a day. The result is projects are significantly delayed and sometimes never even completed.

So how do we stop squirrel syndrome? Or shiny object syndrome?

Turn off all the notifications!

- Phone
- Email
- Calendar
- Social media
- RSS feeds
- Smartwatch
- Messenger apps
- App update requests
- Every blinking light, ding, bing, and whistle that will grab your attention

Try **unsubscribing** from things you do not need. A great time to do this is when you come back from a holiday and everything has piled up in your inbox. Easy to sort and unsubscribe in a batch setting with all those emails in your inbox! I always look forward to this task when I get home. It means less email in the weeks to come!

Time Budgeting:

Let's talk about time management. Time is a finite resource, you cannot make more of it, and once you have spent it, it's gone forever. It is too precious to waste or misuse. So let's get in control of how you plan and spend your time, so you never miss anything of value to you or your family.

Sunday Night Planning:

Every Sunday night, I look over the projects on my list and prioritize them, and then assign a time allotment to each one for completion. This gives me great insight into how many hours of work I have in front of me and if the ask is realistic. If it is not, I go back to prioritizing again. I do this until the time required for my week makes sense.

This prioritizing has to include everything in the week: personal goals, family goals, relationship goals, and work goals. Every week I have to touch each one of these areas to make sure I achieve what I want for myself in the long run. Include tasks the household needs you to run, times when your partner and family rely on you – this includes driving and cooking meals!

Remember those three gathering places? You also need to schedule time to process the accumulation in those areas too – everything into the calendar. Don't forget to schedule yourself free time too – that way you know you will enjoy it when you arrive at that time block!

Here is a tool to help you prioritize until you are able to work through it faster with practice:

General Eisenhower developed a decision-making matrix to help him prioritize his focus. That has been layered here with some learning from Darren Hardy.

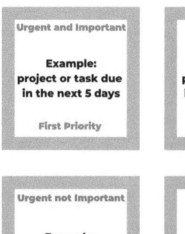

Back to that Sunday night organization time: I have a digital calendar (Google) and a paper calendar (Erin Condren – such a good one!). I transfer from my digital calendar to paper everything that has a hard and fast time to it. Everything that is not flexible goes in first. Then I add in all my family and personal commitments because those are also immovable. I never hear the end when those get goofed up.

I list the projects in order of priority and the hours they need in the left margin. Then I start working the focused time into my calendar in the open spaces for these projects.

Do not step into the pitfall of being a "time optimist." If it is not in your calendar – you will not get it done. This includes travel time. – You need to include that in your calendar too! Colour-code your personal, work, and family. Of course, do not forget to schedule time in for your goals. If you don't work it in, you can't be upset when another year rolls by with no movement on that Big Dreamy Goal of yours!

Now that your time for the week has been carefully laid out – STICK TO IT! You owe it to yourself to not waste all that time you spent planning your precious resource of time! Look ahead and adjust for speed bumps. Do not get totally derailed by Tuesday morning or even Monday afternoon. Be honest about the time things really take; the person who loses out is you and maybe the people you love the most... Those are big stakes and big reasons to get this right!

If you are doing all of these steps I outlined, things should be great, right?

Not so fast! Now we have to talk about the external factors that get in the way of our beautiful colour-coded calendars. Some huge time hijackers are lurking around every water cooler and doorway, just waiting to throw a wrench into your well-laid meticulous plans.

- Interruptions
- Waiting for others who are holding up your project
- The dreaded open-door policy that invites endless interruptions
- Collaborative interruptions
- Peer interactions
- Free webinars that promise amazing results

So how can you handle the unexpected and still protect your valuable time and schedule?

Do you have an open door?

Set hours for it and post on the closed door when you can be interrupted next.

Do you have to collaborate on a project?

Set time aside to do it with a clear start and finish time. Make sure it is in your calendar.

Do you have dedicated uninterrupted time?

> Give yourself at least 90 minutes every day without interruption—you will be shocked at what gets done—no phone, no notifications, etc.

Be mindful of the education you sign up for.

> Those free seminars may actually be stealing your valuable time.
> They come with multiple emails and extended time-sucking activities.

What time of day are you most productive? USE IT!

> What is your natural business-day cycle?
> Usually a.m. is proactive and p.m. is reactive, so the best-focused work gets done in the morning.

Season of life matters too: What season are you in?

> Do you have kids?
> Little kids at home that need you?
> Older kids or empty nest?
> Scale your expectations to match the season of life you are in

In your pursuit of productivity, you should reduce the negative information and influences you consume. Limit social media and the news. Get rid of all those notifications. Consume positive information – podcasts about topics you want to learn about or are interested in. Finding the holy grail of productivity is figuring out how to hack those bad habits and build yourself a framework to be successful.

Home-Life Support

There is no place like home.

L. Frank Baum

The biggest system of support for any entrepreneur is home support. I have lived through not having the support at home. I had a partner who believed they were supportive, but each time work was in the way of his vision, each time I needed an extra hand, the support eroded. What I had was conditional support. The view of: "This is great so long as your work never interrupts my needs." Without my partner unconditionally cheering me on, things fell apart pretty quickly. I tried to ensure he was never inconvenienced by my work schedule or demands. I started to hide things I would normally have shared out of fear of reprisal. I worked ludicrous ways to try and get it done, all while trying to protect a home life that wouldn't protect me. I drove myself into the ground. Over time I became very lonely and scared. It made me confrontational and argumentative. Through it all, I have never once doubted that I would be able to pull through, but I found lots of people along the way who were not worthy of my inner circle.

It is challenging to bring your business to life if you do not have a support system at home to help you get there. We need friends who cheer us on, even when they may miss us in the start-up phase. We need partners who understand our drive and desire to build something from where there was nothing. Partners who understand the sacrifice needed to support a dream and who positively show up when and however they are needed.

If you have ever tried to start a business during the season of small children, you need child care backup. You need school pickup safety nets and dinner fairies to swoop in and save the day.

Not everyone in your support network will be positive. You may start to feel some naysayers enter your life when you are "late again" or you "can't shut it off." In the staffing chapter, chapter five, we discussed the idea of patriots and mercenaries in the workplace. Here is a reminder of the content from Steve Chandler:

> **Patriots** *are the employees who are on the same mission as you. They love what they do. They are servant–leadership-driven. They are proud and committed to the company and the values in place. But most importantly, they are driven to ensure the mission and vision*

are at the forefront of their work. **Mercenaries** *are employees who are there for the paycheque and the personal glory. They are not team players. They tend to break the rules. They tend to do things and ask for forgiveness after. And they are not concerned about their choices and their interactions and how they affect the other employees. They're there for their personal glory.*

We can see this in our personal support systems too. A patriot understands there may be late nights or bungled schedules, and they will still be there cheering you on toward your dream. They know that this is your opportunity, and they want to see you be successful. They help you when you falter, they pick up what you are dropping, and they love you anyway. They make sure dinner is waiting, even when it is way too late to expect it.

A mercenary will prey on your fears. They serve up the guilt trips. They will remind you over and over again how you have let them or the family down once again. They never let you recover from disappointing them and never miss an opportunity to tell you how this will never work and why do you want to do this anyway? They make you feel less-than for wanting something that takes away from their time with you. They get angry when you talk about it again. They will never show you respect for the courage of what you do every day.

Today I have an unconditional support system. Someone who believes in me more than I believe in myself at times. When you have that, it is much easier to take the hits that entrepreneurial life serves up. The home support I enjoy now is incredibly different from my previous relationship. My ups and downs at work do not change the love I receive at the end of the workday. I have friends who don't take it personally when certain times of year I just am not available. They hug me and take me up on a glass of wine when the time is right, without judgment. This life is much healthier than my past experience.

Take a look around you to ensure that you have a support system that wants to see you succeed—people who cheer you on and will provide an ear on a bad day. It matters that you come home at night to a safe space that is nurturing and respectful, not one that provides more stress.

Share

Here are a few of the tools that I have been using in my life to help make things better.

Google Suite – Calendar, Drive, Email, etc. Having all my tools in one place has been helpful. I even have several emails for all my companies pointed to one inbox where I can access all my signatures.

I also use Boomerang as a feature on my email. It allows me to send emails into the future. I can write a reply to that email and schedule it to send tomorrow or next week. I can also send reminders to my staff in the future too. It saves so much time and teaches people when I am in email and available. I might reply at midnight, but it will be sent tomorrow morning, so you do not know my actual working hours.

I use 2 Houses as a way to track finances and calendars with my girl's dad. This also integrates with Google – yay!

I have made my own dashboard in Google Sites. It is a website that has everything I need for all my businesses and household quick-link buttons to banking, health plan submissions, kids' school logins, and more. The only thing I need open on my desktop is this website, and from there, I can navigate in one click to everything else.

I use Google Home in the kitchen. It is synced to my shopping lists. Everyone in the house can yell out to Google to add something to the list. This has made shopping so much less work.

Cleaners. I have a cleaning company and a dog yard pickup service. Yes, I could do it myself. Yes, my mom gives me side-eye over this; however, my time is better spent working on my enterprises and being with my family than it is on these tasks. My justification is: if my dollar per hour work is higher than what I spend on hiring the help, then I hire the help.

I use ASANA at work for task management and I have added my personal tasks as well. I am able to add things like changing furnace filters and annual doctor's appointments, etc. Reminders of the house maintenance needed and personal tasks all go in one tool, and I see it all every day.

Meal planning. Let's face it: entrepreneur life is busy. When I was on my own with my two girls, I loved the meal prep boxes. It was pure gold having three meals delivered to my door that could be prepped quickly, that everyone loved, and that I didn't have to think about! Now that the girls are older, I am having them help out and learn life skills at the same time.

Action Item

Get out a notepad and work through every place you have information.
   Now work through your list to narrow it down to these six places:
- *Physical Inbox*
- *Portable inbox – travels with you*
- *Email inbox – just one*
- *Voicemail – just one*
- *Note pad – paper or digital*
- *Wild card – if what you need is not mentioned*

Action Item

Get out a notepad and make a list of all the places in your life that you face challenges—things like cleaning, meal prep, driving etc. Then take some time to envision what is needed to make it better. It could be a hired service for meals or perhaps an afternoon spent reorganizing the pantry for more efficiency. Not all solutions are expensive. They require creativity.

CHAPTER 9 – EXPANSION

> *Every success story is a tale of constant adaptation, revision and change.*

> *Richard Branson*

If it works once, why not twice? Or three times?

In 2005, the writing was on the wall that rents would be skyrocketing in our market and if we were ever going to get ahead, we would need to consider our location and lease vs own. In 2008, I would be renewing my studio lease and exercising my five-year option. We started to research a second location. We were not clear if we would relocate to it or build an actual second location. We set about looking for locations and exploring rents as well as locations for purchase.

I opened a second location in another city. I managed to secure a private lender and there I was, owner of two locations and now some commercial property that needed to be built out. I had done that before, the build-out I mean, but this time was different. I would do less of it myself, and we would hire more of it out. I was busy, you see, running two locations. I couldn't also be the carpenter and painter. Surely, duplicating the systems we had in place would be sufficient.

I was slowly falling into the trap that false success can build for you. I did less research the second time around. I started to delegate not because I knew what I expected but from overwhelm. I delegated tasks but not outcomes. I did not explain my end goal or what complete looked like. The second buildout was outrageous in cost compared to my first. I was too busy to do it myself or to oversee it well. I already had a successful school that needed my attention. I hired help to build the second location, and it set me up for huge failure right out of the gates.

My desire to pay for more and babysit the project less came back to haunt me. The contractor was the same guy I had used for the first location, but this time I confidently told him that I would need him to build the floors, paint, and take on many of the things we had done ourselves to save money the first time. I did not have the same time wealth with this buildout, and I was prepared to pay, as my private investor had loaned me enough to make it happen.

The contractor talked me into fancy features that we never needed, and we paid dearly for. We built a beautiful Brazilian walnut hardwood floor that was easily over $50,000 – a gregarious buildout – only to discover four months into operations that he hadn't installed humidity, and the floors split and were slicing people's feet open. We were not able to afford to add in the humidity after the fact, and so the beautiful floors were covered by a rubberized option from Sport Court because that is all we could afford. It is a sin that the beautiful floor is still covered up to this day.

This was not our only mistake. I thought I was clever by doing small payouts as the job moved along. My mistake in this was that I was not checking to make sure the vendors were getting paid along the way when I was paying the contractor. Sadly, the same general contractor who did a wonderful job on my first buildout was now pocketing money that belonged to the vendors. Before long, I ended up with liens placed by several contractors, preventing me from getting my occupation permit and preventing us from opening and getting those first few students into class. Now I had to clear the liens in order to open for business. I had used more money than I should have and did not have enough left to fight the scenario I found myself in. It was highly stressful to get the liens cleared and get the blame squarely back where it belonged – on the contractor.

The naivety I had with the success of the first location was my blind spot. I had no idea how "lucky" the success was at the first location. We opened with 230 kids, which I now know is a big school. It seemed to have happened with the skill set I had. I thought I had done all the work with the second location – similar demographics, growing neighbourhoods, good stats for house-hold earnings. I did not count on the one thing that our first loca-tion had without my knowing it – precedent. The first location was in an area where people would try things just to try. They did not need a referral to give something a try. The second location was a small city that still thought of itself as a town. Where no one tries your service unless they were told by a friend. Well, it took over three years to grow to the size of our first location when it had opened. It was devastating to have the same model and same learn-ing and then realize you missed a huge piece of the puzzle because you do not live where your customers live. You do not know where they hang out because you don't hang out there. It was a huge lesson in not just thinking that you know your market on paper, but that you have to go and experience your market and find out how they think. Both locations look similar on paper for demographics, etc., but they have distinct personalities. A lesson I would learn again later in my journey with my third location.

I believed that, because I had been in business for three years with my first location, surely my systems could just be duplicated and run again at the second location. I thought that if I could ask my teachers to teach the same classes at the second location, by having the same staff rotating teaching the same thing with the same systems, we would be brilliant. Wrong. Nothing duplicated well. I thought the website, marketing, payroll, etc. would just be one expense for both locations. There should be savings by running two spaces. All my research told me this should be the case.

None of this was true. We incorporated a second company, thinking we were protecting each asset separately – having received this advice. What this single decision meant was that all the savings you think you have by just using the same services you already purchased did not work. There were now two sets of books, two sets of bank accounts and credit cards, two filings for taxes, two merchant machine accounts, two phone accounts… The list goes on. The single decision to incorporate a second company negated all the savings we might have found. It would be three years until we were able to find the right lawyer to amalgamate the companies into one, and then there was a substantial cost to that along with merging the books to create a chart of accounts that made sense and could provide helpful data. Back to the same point as earlier – you need to find the right people at the right time. I thought I had learned from my first mistake of trying to incorporate my own company, but I was led astray again on the legal and bookkeeping consequences of what we were doing. We thought it was clever to keep each location as its own entity so it would be easy to show the worth of the company if we ever sold it. You don't need all the fees of two companies to do that – you need a bookkeeper who knows what they are doing.

Once we moved past the mess of the back-end operations, we looked at staffing. It turns out that the staff did not want to work at both locations. Some took exception to driving that far north, so now I had some teachers teaching at both and some at only one. All of a sudden, the logistics of staff meetings got complicated – everything needed to be hosted twice. Rather than having a strong teaching team that made the same programming happen strongly at both locations, I was hosting several trainings and meetings, most often twice, because staff refused to travel to the other location if it was not where they typically worked their hours.

As the locations began to grow their own distinct personalities, the management of them quickly outgrew not just my bandwidth of hours in a day but my skill set too. I was being challenged on my policies every time I turned around. It was incredibly difficult, and most days were spent in the whirlwind of overwhelm. Fourteen-to-sixteen-hour days became the norm, and I had two young kids at home. My family began to suffer and of course my marriage. The studio became the third person in our relationship. Always there, ready to hijack any moment. What is hard about overwhelm is that your loved ones don't know how to help you fix it and you're so far in, you cannot see the forest through the trees to find your way out. This is where having a coach, mentor, or networking group becomes so crucial. You need someone who is not emotionally involved to take a bird's-eye view and help you work your way out of the forest safely.

Unfortunately, at this time, I had the wrong networking group. I had joined, and my husband at the time, encouraged it. He said something that has stuck with me for many years: Successful people surround themselves with successful people. This is the room you need to be in if you want to level up your game. So I joined with money I didn't have to make "friends" who didn't really care about my success. This group was full of people who were posing as more successful than they were. This resulted in my taking advice from people who I thought had great insights and solid advice. I made a lot of bold decisions, thinking I was wise. I was just being led down the wrong path by people who would never help me live through the consequences of the advice they gave.

A Third Location

You can't build out a single room for that price! How could you not do it?

Unnamed Networking Group Attendee

We had barely gotten the second location off the ground when I was in a car accident. In an instant my life changed forever. At the time I had been teaching 35 hours a week and managing 30 hours a week. I went from full throttle to nothing.

In that single moment, I lost my ability to teach, my creative outlet, my passion, my physical exercise, and my ability to blow off steam. My third place.

We all grow up with home and school, and those of us who are really lucky find a third place. A place where we get to start our day over again, where we are accepted for who and what we are where we are at. A separate group of peers who give you grace that your school peers can't or won't. If we are really lucky, that third place may even turn into a career that doesn't feel like work, that you would do for free. It's not about the paycheque; it is about a calling. That is how my life unfolded. I know I am one of the lucky ones—that I get to play at my work. My work is a calling and a blessing, and I have so much gratitude for everything the arts have provided both to my family and to me.

Now that the car accident had changed my life, I was reeling. Being unable to teach, I had to hire more teachers to take my hours, and that was an increase to payroll. Now that I had 35 more hours out of my week because I was no longer teaching, I found I needed more to do. I did not give the time back to my family or even to myself for injury recovery. I looked for ways to fill it with other things. I had increased payroll to cover. This too would become a regret.

I became aware of a studio for sale in the south end of Calgary. After further research, it seemed too good to be true. And as they say, if it seems too good to be true, it probably is. I took this to my networking group at the time and the business coach leading it.

This is what my peers in my networking group were saying: "No brainer." – "How could you not do it?"

I know how you can "not" do it – your finances tell you that you do not have this figured out yet. You get a mentor that gives you just enough knowledge to be dangerous, and BAM! You have yourself a third location that your books don't support and that you have not learned how to do the due diligence on or the resources to hire someone to help do the research properly.

The reasons to do it were piled high around me. I had few reasons to walk away from the opportunity. My husband at the time was not too excited about the opportunity. I see now that he really had little understanding about how the injuries of the car accident had affected my ability to feel relevant. He failed to see that I was struggling without my identity as a teacher. Had he seen it and been able to help me when I was unable to help myself, maybe the outcome would have been different. Instead he said: "If you can find the money, but it is not coming from our family savings." Challenge accepted.

I hit the ground running; I made a new business plan. I made new five-year projections, with new research into the market. My mentor taught me how to shop it to a bank, as this would be my first loan that was not from a private lender. I went to three banks and was turned down. I became focused on changing the no into a yes more than I focused on the business I was buying. That blind spot would come back to haunt me in a few short months.

I managed to convince the bank that I do most of my banking with to give me the $50,000 to purchase and renovate the space to match our other location's branding. Much to my husband's surprise, I got the loan without his help and, as it would turn out, without his blessing. He should have said no, which is what he was actually thinking. He never thought I would be successful in getting the money. This would become a wedge in our relationship that we would never overcome.

Hindsight is a beast of a thing. The "coulda-shoulda's" will eat you alive. I should have heard him more clearly. He should have known I would take the challenge. We both should have talked more clearly about what was happening. I needed to feel needed. He needed to feel heard. And with this, we stepped into what would be a terrible outcome for our family.

The people in my networking group were extremely supportive. Many of them had multiple locations or multiple businesses, and they were so positive about why I should.

"You can't build out a room for that price."

"You have systems in place already."

"You already have two locations. It's nothing to add another."

"Now that you are not teaching, you have the time to manage another location."

"You would be the largest dance school in Calgary and surrounding area."

Not one of these people asked me if I did the market research as I had done with the other two locations. No one asked if I knew how to do my due diligence properly. I did not ask if anyone had bought an existing business before and the pitfalls to watch out for. Not a single soul in this group of "successful owners" asked me questions that would challenge me and poke holes, to ensure it was a good decision. This is why I say that even though successful people surround themselves with successful people, if these people are issuing huge advice for big changes, make sure they show up in your life more than a couple of times a year. My current networking group and small mastermind group would never have let this opportunity pass the "sniff test." My current group of people would have had me asking good questions, and this learning would never have happened.

Sadly, I did not have good advisors in my life at that time, and I bulldozed my headstrong way into this opportunity. I bought the studio. We made the decision to allow the current owner to finish the year they had promised their students, so the transition would be smooth. This was the biggest mistake of my professional career to date.

I thought I was buying a turnkey operation that was barely profitable. I signed a new five-year lease. It had two dance rooms built out already with mirrors, sprung floors, and barres. The lobby needed about $10k in renovations to bring it up to the standard of our brand.

What I really bought that April was a studio that had 180 people on the client list (which was actually 150 once duplicate accounts were removed) and the space contents. The staff had indicated they would likely stay if new contracts were offered.

The staff became lazy, customer service dropped, and the clients were led to believe it was because of new management. It was actually because the person who sold it to me started to provide less service, the staff cared less about their jobs, and I had no guidance on how to take on a company that I had not built from scratch. "From scratch" and "purchase" are two such different scenarios.

When it came time for the students to reregister, exactly **four students** returned out of the 180 we thought we had purchased. Complete devastation. What happened? Where did they all go? I thought I was taking crazy pills. Then one brave soul took pity on me while I was calling them to ask if they would be returning.

"No, we won't be. The new management company did not give us a great end-of-year experience. The teachers were sitting while teaching, classes started late and ended early, and we did not get the value for our tuition paid."

I asked if I could have a few more minutes of her time. I knew I had finally found the information that I needed to figure out why this had gone sideways. I explained how we had allowed the previous owner to finish the year and that we were not involved in her complaints at all. She paused and thoughtfully stated, "You will have a hard time getting the word out to change people's minds. But I believe you, and I can tell in your voice that you are sincere."

I offered her two months' free tuition if she would return and more account credit for any students she would bring back with her. Student by student, I rebuilt the third location from what was worse than scratch. We had to overcome a bad reputation that was not mine.

I reached out to my lawyer. Surely the goodwill part of this purchase had been breached. We agreed that we would reach out to the other party and suggest the final payment was not appropriate given what we had uncovered. The other party replied with the intention to sue for defamation of character and, "Yes. You will make the final payment as agreed." Wow. This would be my first foray into legal territory and uncharted waters.

I continued to slowly and steadily implement what I could to get students through the door at that location. I licked my wounds financially. I fell into such debt that I started waking at night in cold sweats. I was panicking and moving money every day to avoid bouncing payments and hiding how bad things were from my disapproving husband. He was not on board, and even though he had some of the skills I lacked and he could have helped, his attitude toward me had changed. It chased my problems and ability to speak to him underground. He was constantly critical of me, and it chipped away at my spirit and self-esteem more than he will ever know.

I was suffering from depression from my accident and from the financial business hole I had dug myself. My husband would tell me that I was lazy and not injured, and to get up and get out of the house and get back to work. The thing about depression is that you can't see it. It silently steals away your strength and courage. It slowly keeps you home, away from the people you need most. Once you have isolated yourself, it takes over and even the task of getting out of bed can zap your energy for the day. Add in the chronic pain from my injuries and I had little capability to manage myself well. I had a four-year-old and a one-year-old, and three locations, two dogs, and a home to run. I could not find my way any longer.

When I entered marriage, I believed it was forever, through sickness and in health, through the good and the bad. I never believed the person I chose would not keep the same promise. I had thought it was about lifting each other up to be the best we could be, together. The communication breakdown we experienced with the purchase of the third location would continue to drive a wedge between us that I was not capable of seeing. My health issues were piling up. He asked me to go on medication. I hadn't wanted to, but I thought he was making a decision to help me when I could not help myself. I knew I was not well, and I trusted him. Turns out I was wrong.

In my new medicated state, I was too groggy in the morning to get my oldest to school. I was too injured to lift my youngest from her crib when she needed me. I was hazy all day from pain meds and completely knocked out at night with sleep aids. I became a zombie. I have few memories of my youngest as a toddler. I spent those two years in a medicated haze, and I regret that so much. He continued to accuse me of being lazy and that I needed to get up and do better. I spiralled. He demanded we sue the other driver. Now I was in an injury lawsuit to add to what I could not handle.

I would go to physiotherapy, the pain clinic, spinal injections, neck injections, and counselling, day in and day out. At every appointment, I was reliving how this impacted my life—having to outline how negative it all was. I believe this is a problem in our health system. My injury lawsuit required regular appointments to keep the file updated and relevant. For two years, I made appointments that I didn't want, getting no results, just more pain meds, more anti-depression meds, more sleep meds, meds for the side effects. For two years, 4-5 days a week, I would be required to talk about all the negative things that this accident had caused in my life. No wonder people don't get better if you have to stay in the negative. I was done. I hated it all. I kept asking the pain clinic what the exit plan was. I was too young at 34 to be living this way for the rest of my life. I was eventually kicked out of the pain clinic for being a difficult patient. All I wanted was an end to the insanity. I was doing the same thing every day and getting the same result, hoping for something different.

We went on a family trip to Hawaii in November of 2012. It was a nine-day cruise of the islands with our girls and my networking group. I was so excited to get away from my regular schedule of appointments. I even planned to go off my meds that trip (I did not seek medical advice to do this, and I would never recommend this to anyone). I wanted to remember every moment of it. Unbeknownst to me, it would be our last vacation together as a family.

He was so angry during that holiday. At every expense, he would get frustrated. He never relaxed. He wouldn't speak to me. Meanwhile, I was going through crazy withdrawal and was grateful for the motion of the ship to hide my symptoms. I have wonderful memories of my girls playing on the beaches, seeing the sea life, enjoying the ship and the dinners. What I still can't reconcile is that we had many moments together and the child care that should have provided my husband and I with time to reconnect, but it just couldn't happen. I still don't know how he felt about the trip. I believe all he saw was a price tag and a wife he no longer loved or knew how to connect with. Somewhere along the way, he forgot the promise he made to me of forever, in front of our family and friends and God. That Christmas, we had a huge argument that tilted my world's axis. It would never be the same again.

December 15, 2012. The night we fought. The second time I feared for my personal safety with him. I left the party before it began and robotically drove home. I took off my rings and cried myself into a fitful sleep. I went to the mall early the next day to return all the Christmas gifts that he was angry I had bought. I returned the dress that I didn't wear to the party the night before. I asked my parents to keep the kids an extra night. He came home and berated me again. Demanded to know where the kids were, furiously packed a bag and disappeared for several days. Then it was Christmas. We had family fly in, I did my best to present things were fine, but inside I was feeling things for the first time in years, as I was no longer taking any medication. I was falling to pieces.

I continued to work at my business, now realizing I had no fallback plan. I had no option to not take an income, as I was now truly alone for the first time in my life. I entered 2013 scared to my core. Never had I felt so useless, alone, unworthy, and such a failure in so many aspects. All the things he had been telling me showed themselves to be true. The overachiever had failed, and I had no skills to pick myself up.

I became a recluse. I cried on my knees every day after he left for work, begging God to end it all, asking for guidance, pleading, bargaining. Then I would get off my knees by the grace of God, dry my tears, and take one step at a time to get through my day.

He came and went for three months. When he was home, he lived in the basement. He lied to the kids about where he was and what he was doing, faking normalcy. He became something I could no longer recognize. Hate seeped out from under the basement door when he was home. It would become a space I would never feel comfortable in again. He moved out, and the pain got deeper like I never thought it could. The day my kids spent their first night at his new place (he never did tell me where it was), I thought my heart would bleed out and I would never heal.

But I got up. Every day. I cried on my knees, begged for help from a God that I felt abandoned by, dried my tears, and put one foot in front of the other. I had 29 cents in the bank, and for the first time in forever, I could feel something burning inside me. Passion was returning. I was living on my own for the first time at age 35. I had always let him manage the finances at home because I was stretched enough with the studio. I realized I had no idea how much the house cost to run. When were the bills due? I wasn't even on the accounts. I had a steep learning curve and two huge reasons to figure it out quickly: my two girls. They needed me to figure it out and make sense of our house and my business.

One thing we were never able to do together was to create a budget. Instead, I was always told, "This is how much we will spend." It was never a joint decision, and that is why we could never agree on money. I have since done the Dave Ramsey Financial Peace course and hired a financial coach, and I, the person who was never capable of a budget before, I who was told, "You don't know the value of a dollar," managed just fine to live on a budget and to save quite easily. It turns out I just want to be an equal partner in those decisions, not have them dictated to me. As the buyer in the household, I believe the tables were tilted. I bought groceries, I bought clothing for the girls, and I wrote cheques for lessons, preschool, and piano. It seemed like I was excessive, and at times I may have been, but 95% of the time it was the cost of the life we built – not my inability to understand the value of money and how it should be spent.

It is no surprise that women control the majority of wallet decisions in a household. Various reports have said 85 – 93% of purchases are controlled by women (Yankelovich Monitor & Greenfield Online). If up to 93% of all transactions worldwide are controlled by women, you can see that women make our world economy turn. They are doing what I did. Purchasing for the household, making the buying decisions. How many times have you been in a store where the man turns to his partner and says, "I like it, but what do you think?" If the woman doesn't like it, the transaction doesn't happen. To have my husband enjoy that I did those tasks for the house, and then be belittled for it, was difficult and hard to reconcile.

I was on my own for the first time in my life, responsible for a household that I would never have acquired if I had been on my own. I had two kids that didn't have a say in the separated parents they now had. They needed me to hold myself to a higher standard than I ever had. Every decision I made for the next five years would be run through a filter of how this would affect our life and if it was the best decision and outcome I could make for them. I made a promise that they would never see me sweat their father and my healing journey from emotional abuse. They should be allowed to see him as he truly was to them, and time would reveal to them what they needed to know. It would not be me that shaped that feeling for them.

This was, as he had said many times to me, "my mess," and I intended to clean up and make something amazing out of less than nothing.

This is how I started to see that my networking group was not the right one. But there were no other options. I could not see anything inside our industry that would serve me better. I took advice from people who were not in the trenches with me. They gave the advice to make a big change without knowing the whole picture. In fact, they made me feel silly for even questioning the purchase: "Just do it." They did not know the whole picture, and I am not sure I ever would have told them. I was aware I was in a room of pretenders at these events. Everyone pretending to be bigger and better than they were, so much imposter syndrome in that room. These people would likely have never given this advice or done this deal themselves had they known all the details of my financial state, my personal health, or my marriage. I believe that they are good people who don't realize the impact of their casual advice. But as Jim Rohn says, "Casualness causes casualties." I became a casualty of the advice and decisions that I made as a result.

I think it is important to note that no one made me make these choices. They were all mine and mine alone. I was not forced, but I did look for guidance from people I admired and believed they would not steer me wrong. I have since joined a networking group that serves me better, and my hindsight allows me to see that no one asked the right questions, least of all me, and I was the one making the decision.

It is important to have people who play devil's advocate on big decisions and someone you will listen to even if it's painful. Somewhere between starting the business and getting to year seven, those people were no longer in my life. I had stopped reading and learning and started coasting because that was all I had the capacity for. Had my mentor at the time or my peers really known me, they would have seen that I was already struggling way too much daily and that a third location was not a good decision. It was an ego project, and those are never good choices.

Never take advice from people you don't talk to regularly or who don't know the whole story so they can advise properly. If you are going to get life-changing advice, make sure your tribe has the same vibe, that you all stand on the same values. Make sure you have people that will tell it to you straight and that you will hear them. Not where everybody is pretending to be something they're not.

When to Expand:

You will either step forward into growth or you will step back into safety.

Abraham Maslow

All of this information serves to say that expansion can be problematic, but it can also be an amazing opportunity when the circumstances are evaluated properly. So how do we know when we are ready to expand?

We know that our systems will break every multiple of 250 customers we serve. We also know that we need robust documentation of the systems and processes that our business uses in order to duplicate them at a second or third location.

Another consideration is that each location, while it may be governed by the same software and systems, maybe even some of the same staff, will each have its own culture due to the clientele you serve there. No matter how much you replicate, you will always need to serve the culture and the community's unique needs.

When your current location is operating at 85% or more of capacity, you should be considering expansion. If you have been looking at your finances all along, that is when your company growth should be able to sustain the addition of space and resources.

So while I had an unlucky expansion to three locations, I did have a successful expansion of my second location in 2018, where we obtained more space after running several years at 90% capacity. When done right, the expansion works well and serves the company and the clients. When done poorly, the strain on resources can be catastrophic. I also had that experience and am grateful to be on the other side of it now.

When to Downsize or Close Locations

*Just because you can open more locations
doesn't mean you should.*

Tara Pickford

With expansion we also need to consider when to offload or close a location. Just like we have to evaluate when a program or service is no longer hitting the numbers to keep providing it, you may need to close a location.

I closed two locations in 2013 as a result of my separation and a couple of other factors. My very first location had been open for 10 years and had been very successful until we had a staff person who took students with them when they left for a new location. Alongside that difficult scenario, we also had a landlord that was refusing to answer calls regarding renewing the lease. I had made another mistake: when we executed our five-year option, I had not ensured there were another five years in the agreement available to us. Now a location that was struggling to meet its financial obligations was also out of a home.

I could look for a new location or close-up shop. Given the absolute strain I was under financially, there was absolutely no way to pay for a buildout and move. The writing was on the wall. We closed and looked to sell our remaining student list to other local studios and entice students to our other location 15 minutes away.

Now we had the third location to evaluate. It had taken two years since the purchase to make it financially viable after the terrible handoff we had from the previous owner. I had found another studio owner who was interested in a turnkey operation. Because it had just broken even the previous month and I needed to get things off my plate, the deal was: "Just take over the lease and here is your turnkey operation." No money to invest; just carry on operations under your own name.

Back to: "If it seems too good to be true, it usually is." This person signed the lease behind me. Meaning that if they didn't pay, I would be responsible. I had prepaid their two summer months of rent, and they were to take over in September, the best time of year to gain new students. Well, they never opened that fall and never made a rent payment, leaving me on the hook for $90,000 in rent (three years remaining on the lease) due immediately due to non-payment. Even worse is that all the students that we had worked so hard to gain were all gone too by the time we were made aware of the problem. Now we had a huge debt to pay and no students to work with. It was a huge disaster.

In the end, I made a deal with the owner to pay the amount owing over four years or to claim bankruptcy and he would receive no payments. He accepted my terms. I went after the studio owner for the amount defaulted on, with very limited success. It is so expensive to go after someone, and in the meantime, I had a bill to keep paying to the owner to prevent another lawsuit from that angle.

All this to say that, in hindsight, just because you can expand doesn't mean you should. There are many factors to look into. I have coached many clients on expansion, drawing on my pitfalls, to help shape the right questions to ask before jumping in. There are many scenarios where expansion is the right choice. I expanded five years after all these terrible scenarios happened. With the right information and due diligence, expansion can be amazing for your company.

Action Item – Expansion

Are you ready to expand?

- *Calculate your usage of space. Look at all the spaces available in a classroom, all the potential class times. How many units are you bringing in? How many units are available to sell?*
- *Are you using 85% of your capacity consistently?*
- *Do the work to see if your market can support an expansion, and think about how big that expansion needs to be.*
- *Is it one room? Or two rooms? More?*
- *Think about the buildout costs to move; there will be a period of time where cash flow is tight because of the expansion.*
- *How much do you need to save up?*
- *How can you mitigate that?*
- *How far will your clients travel to a new/different location?*

If you are at 70-80%, it is time to start considering what moves are available to you.

If you are at 80-85%, it is time to start actively making plans.

If you are at 85% or more consistently, then it might be time to make that healthy business grow.

CHAPTER 10 – STAFFING 2.0

If you look after your staff, they'll look after your customers. It's that simple.

Richard Branson

Previously we talked about the beginnings of hiring people, how you often hire people you know and what happens when those hires are no longer the right ones for your growing business. As your business matures, you start to see that **the people you start with are not the people you will finish with.** This makes complete sense. Often the owner of the business will grow at a much more rapid pace than the staff they hire, and eventually, they come to a crossroads. So what can we do to ensure that the growth we have in mind for ourselves and our business is not stifled by people who do not grow as fast as we need them to?

In my experience, this happened the hard way a couple of times. My dad, who was a very experienced auditor in his own career, upon retiring began to work with me on my books. After a time, it became clear that we have two very different approaches to most things. The problem was that he was my dad, and that was a hard fire. I love him dearly, but at this time, he was stunting my growth. He had to leave in order for me to learn and grow at the speed that I wanted and needed to. I invited both him and my mom to a fancy steak restaurant. When the waiter asked if we were celebrating anything, I announced, "Yes, my father's second retirement!" Then I slid a card across the table. It was not my most gracious moment, but what a relief to finally remove the daily conflict from my business life.

Examine Your Hiring Practices

In looking for people to hire, look for three qualities: integrity, intelligence and energy. And if they don't have the first, the other two will kill you.

Warren Buffett

What can we do at the start of the process to ensure the candidate really is a good fit for our company? In Chapter Four, we talked about asking for detailed information from the start. This process can also go much deeper. You are setting the expectations from the start. If you have a robust interview process, but then their first day is spent standing around the water cooler and going for long lunches – what tone have you set? If you do not set the pace right from the start, you have lost the opportunity to get them running beside you in growth, rather than dragging behind you, never catching up.

We only get the first 90 days with an employee once. Make the most of it! Be ready for them on their first day. Have some projects for them to get started on. Make an opportunity for them to shine in front of their peers so they can be accepted into the fold right away. Set the independent work expectations immediately. Then teach them that failure is okay so long as it was in an attempt to grow and there were learnings. **Face the situation, collect the lessons, and grow forward.**

Encourage their strengths and set them up to succeed. Teach them not to bring you problems without also bringing some solutions. Don't rescue them. Let them learn and grow and have autonomy for their position and choices. Teach them how to run beside you all the time. The purpose of having staff and teammates is to lighten the load, so don't hire people who need micromanaging and don't over-manage those you hire. Employees don't lack potential—they lack leaders who lead with clarity and expectations.

I used to have a terrible first day planned for people. They would come to work, and all through the time talking to them, I would realize another thing we didn't have ready for them. No key for the door, no alarm code, no time sheet set up – oh, yeah, I will have to make a copy of that for you. No staff clothing in their size. The list goes on. I am sure that anyone who I hired back in my beginning days was wondering if we were really ready for them at all.

Now we have a template where there are several people involved in getting prepared for the new hire's starting day, and instructions for who the hire meets their first day and what to cover before their first shift is done. Then we have a list of items to be done before they complete their first week. It is a much different experience now, being hired to work for me. I now get compliments from the new hires that the process was so smooth and they already feel like they belong. That's a huge win because the sooner that hire hits the ground running, the sooner they are making an impact that benefits us all.

Review Contracts

It is impossible to unsign a contract, so do all your thinking before you sign.

Warren Buffett

Once you start to hire those A-level employees, you need to ensure your contracts are clearly in place. Hiring a human resources firm is never a bad spend. You can easily spend thousands of dollars on lawyers tweaking contracts, but what you really need is someone who is an expert in employment contracts. That is exactly what HR firms do. Go right to the experts. It matters that these people understand the local laws where you operate from. If you are operating in several jurisdictions, make sure you are covered in each one. This is key because the nuances really do matter. You never know which clause is the one you will be grateful for when issues come up. Make a list of the things that are important to you and your industry. Ensure the contract has a treatment for those items. Contracts are meant to protect both parties. Be sure that it spells it out clearly for everyone involved. Make sure it has enforceable clauses; no point in signing something that can't be enforced.

I have taken many coaching calls from clients who are frustrated that their contracts do not have a clause that covers the scenario they are in. Vicki once asked me how to handle a teacher that turned in her resignation and was now demanding to hold a going-away party for herself for the students to say goodbye. I can tell you that any type of event like this is bad for business if you haven't already lived it. As a business, our goal is to get the next great teacher into the room and help those students as soon as possible. The problem with a staff person who is leaving is that they have stopped looking out for the company mission, and they are now looking out only for themselves. They forget that the rest of the company is still moving forward and will be as soon as they are gone. They will often even forget how previous staff have left and what those impacts looked like. The best thing for retention is to get that teacher out as soon as possible before they have an opportunity to influence students to do anything other than stay in your business.

In Vicki's case, she had no wording around how someone leaves the company, so we worked on adding to her contracts that employees agree to leave on the terms provided by the company upon termination of employment, regardless of the reasons. That upon notice of the end of employment, management will provide clear instructions that must be followed or there will be monetary penalties. This clause needs to be agreed to before employment begins. We can never predict how someone will choose to leave a company that they were once excited to be a part of, so you need to have all the tools in place so you can execute in many ways depending on the scenario.

Handbooks

You should have a handbook that expands on policies and contractual obligations, as well as one that is more of a culture handbook for "The way we do things around here." I am not a lawyer, nor do I play one while authoring this book. You should always ensure that you have proper legal counsel when introducing new policies.

Employee handbooks include policies like:
- Our philosophy
- Code of conduct
- Conflict-of-interest policy
- Dress code policy
- Hours of work, overtime, holidays, and vacation
- Leaves of absence
- Attendance policy and scheduling
- Discipline policy
- Confidentiality
- Drug and alcohol policy
- Internet and email policy
- Termination of employment

You may wish to have a second book that speaks more to your culture:
- Culture laws for your business
- Where to find office supplies and order them
- Where to park
- Giving back
- Key event dates/ closure dates
- Unique treatments of your workplace and environment

All of these manuals lead to policies for everything from having a front-door key to being issued a computer, employee discounts, work from home, security cameras on-site, and use of photography and video. The list goes on. If it happens in your workplace, you need to document it.

Vicki, from our story above, was also missing handbooks for her staff. Her policies were memos that had been sent out over the years, but there was no one place to find them or one place for her employees to look them up along the way. There were times when new hires had never even seen the memos because they weren't around when they were handed out. Through our work together, Vicki and I were able to create one place for all policies and information to be found. Even better, staff were able to look up questions they had before coming to her. They solved issues for themselves. Vicki has mentioned several times how she is much happier with all the tools and policies in one place and how clear everything is for anyone who is asking.

Building Job Descriptions

When you accepted your job, you were not chosen solely to fill a position on the organization chart; you were chosen to fill a responsibility.

David Cottrell

This is always one of those things that get put off and never are completed. **You really should not hire someone if you are not clear on what you are hiring them to do.** If you are hiring them for more than one position, give them a job description for each position that they have been hired for.

What makes for a completed job description? You will also need to complete this for every position in your company. This will help you get clear on what type of person you are trying to hire. A well-rounded job description that ticks all the boxes needs to include the following:

- Job title
- Purpose of the job
- Who they report to
- Anyone who reports to them
- Duties and responsibilities
- How they will be measured for performance – what results are being measured
- Skills required
- Attributes of the successful candidate
- Responsibilities
- Qualifications
- Working conditions description
- Physical requirements – like strength, mobility, vision, hearing
- Psychological demands
- Acknowledgement of and agreement to the above

While we are talking about job descriptions, you will notice one of the requirements for a well-rounded description is how performance will be measured. The key here is to decide how to provide the hire with feedback about how well they are meeting the expectations of the position and ultimately of you as the boss. Another piece of this is to normalize the feedback so that it never comes out of left field.

Your people should know when and how often their performance is being evaluated. Will it be monthly? Every 60 days? Quarterly? Annually? Consider that the more frequent it is, the more often you can effect change in their performance. While it can sometimes be more work to evaluate more frequently, the payoff is also much better. It is human nature to turn up the heat on performance when a review is right around the corner. Harness that natural by-product to help your company excel.

Further to this idea, how will they know when they have been successful enough in the role to earn a reward such as a bonus, a pay raise, or a move up the ladder in their career with you? While setting out the description, you also need to build out the feedback component. Your people should never have feedback they didn't know was coming. It should be clear to everyone what they are being measured against.

Some measurements could be:

- Sales goals
- Retention of customers
- New lead conversions
- Rate of renewed business
- Innovation
- Teamwork
- Customer reviews of interactions
- Accounts receivable
- Time management
- Finished work
- Promotion of company events

From the start, it should be clear to the hire what you will be watching for, so they understand where performance matters. Create a system that allows the employee to evaluate their work and their supervisor to do the same. Then they compare scores and talk through the issues and expectations, setting the framework for the next period of measurement.

This process allows you to goal-set with your people. Without goals, they will not get much done. Having these regular intervals to evaluate goals and set new ones will help you make growth and results part of the culture of your company. Help them set SMART goals:

- Specific
- Measurable
- Achievable
- Relevant
- Time-bound

Every goal needs to have the attributes of a SMART goal.

When I was coaching Melanie on how to build her job descriptions for her boutique fitness studio, we talked a lot about ensuring that the descriptions were clear for each role and how frequently she would be able to evaluate them. In some cases that meant she would need to be able to sit in on classes they taught to help them learn better skills and inform her feedback. Not only did Melanie have to build their job descriptions, but she also had to build out for herself how she would be inspecting the outcomes she expected. She had to think about how frequently they needed feedback—in her case, it was frequently upon hiring and less frequently as time went on in their employment journey—and how she could realistically provide that within her own schedule.

Now Melanie includes the job descriptions and the measurement tools in her hiring contract package, meaning that if an employee has accepted the offer of employment, they already know how they will be evaluated and how frequently. She no longer has the awkwardness of evaluations that seem irregular and more of punishment when they happen. They are now normalized in her culture and used as improvement tools, not ways to write someone up and remove them.

The Vitals

> *You alone are responsible for what you do, don't do, or how you respond to what's done to you.*
>
> *Darren Hardy*

You might have noticed that I have referenced Darren Hardy several times. That is because the training he provides in his higher-level programs creates fundamental truths. He runs a free training every day called the Darren Daily, but I have spent time with him on higher-level training programs that have been invaluable to me, like this next concept on the vitals.

When we go to the hospital, they always measure our vital signs – our heart rate, our blood oxygen levels, our blood pressure, our rate of breathing, and our temperature. This is so that they can find out how well we are doing. It gives them key information about what to treat us for. It does no good to cast the broken arm if I am bleeding out internally. Vitals help us see everything, even those things that are not obvious right away.

In our business, you have several vitals that we can measure:

- Vital functions
- Vital priorities
- Vital metrics
- Vital improvements

Vital functions are skills or processes that cannot be delegated. The business grows because the person in that role is the best person for that job and those tasks are their wheelhouse. When we are determining what roles our company needs, we need to think about why the position is so important and be sure that we are hiring for the skills that the position requires. This is an important clarity moment.

Vital priorities are the three things our role is responsible for. They are the three big goals that our position needs to accomplish in the next 12 months. In fact, we will be successful if we only do these three things, and the position is irrelevant if we don't accomplish them. Vital priorities help us limit the number of decisions we need to make, so we can get to work on the important tasks that we must focus on.

Vital metrics are the ways we measure if the functions and priorities are getting done and if they are, in fact, the correct ones to be working on. This is the way in which we decide to measure what success looks like. It can be a revenue goal, customer number, task management, etc. We need to determine the best way to measure if the vitals are being done, and done well.

Vital improvements are the ways we outline that the job can go the "extra mile." That if we are reaching all our goals and we give just a little bit more, this is what it would look like in that role in the company. For our front desk, it looks like finding more efficiencies, engaging in professional development, or giving the extra touch to our customers.

These all go hand in hand – functions, priorities, metrics, and improvements. They should be talked about together. They also need to be discussed when setting goals within the job description. I have built out an example from our front desk job description.

Front Desk Job Description

Vital Functions – What You Do

1. Database and account management
2. Sales and lead conversion
3. Hospitality

Vital Priorities – How You Do It

1. Timely management of emails and ASANA tasks
2. Timely response to inquiries and lead generation, as well as follow-up procedures
3. Listen to families to look for ways for impact, keep studios in good repair and cleanliness, clean workspace/diffuser, etc.

Vital Metrics – How To Measure It

1. AR – under $2000
2. Student and unit numbers/withdrawals
3. ASANA and email up to date

Vital Improvements – How To Get Better

1. Engage in professional development.
2. Look for systems to improve.
3. Look for ways to go the extra mile.

KRAs and KPIs

> *If you can't measure it, you can't improve it.*
>
> *Peter Drucker*

I mentioned Dave Ramsey previously with Financial Peace University. He also offers *Entreleadership Training*, which inspired this next concept.

Now that we have the skeleton for a job description outlined above let's talk about how you will take those descriptions to the next level.

KRAs or Key Results Areas are the "how" of an employee's job. It is usually three to five must-do tasks for their role. If they don't do that task, no one else in the company will do the job either, and it will thwart progress for the whole company. Use KRAs to evaluate performance in the role and future promotions. These define what winning looks like. **If you do these things, you are winning in your role.** Here is an example for our front desk staff. We also include how to go the "extra mile" because that is something we encourage all the time.

Front Desk KRAs

1. First impressions – Orderliness, cleanliness, professional dress, and smiles
2. Information – Accessible, organized, and accurate
3. Accuracy – Regarding enrollment, accounts, and information
4. Discernment – Knowing when to listen, when to speak up, and when to let go
5. Inquiries – Answering phones within three rings, checking and returning messages promptly, and being cheerful and helpful

Going the extra mile: "How can I help you?" "That's a great question!" "Let me ask around for you." Be friendly and smile.

KPIs or Key Performance Indicators are how you measure progress toward the goal for that job in your company. These are used to measure progress or how effective that person is in their role. Your KRA is the task, and the KPI is the measurement of the task. They are interconnected.

This is a great item to add to performance reviews or to your dashboard if you wish to make radical change happen that you measure more frequently than you do performance reviews.

Raises, Bonuses, and Benefits

The team with the best players usually does win – this is why you need to invest the majority of your time and energy in developing your people.

Jack Welch

Investing in your people will never go wrong. Your team will always go the extra mile if they feel appreciated.

You may discover at some point that creating systems for raises, bonuses, and benefits for employees will help take work off your plate. All of these employee systems take time to manage and administer, but they are important for your employees to feel seen, heard, and cared for. Everyone wants to know that there is the possibility of advancement or a raise in pay. Put systems in place to help guide your decisions. These systems can also be worked into your budgets, further helping you get on top of your company's needs.

Performance Raises should be considered in percentages. According to Indeed, the average performance review raise is 3%. If you are normalizing feedback several times a year, this does not mean you are giving raises every time there is a review. But you can start to predict how many performance reviews lead to enough performance increase to earn a raise.

Another raise that is important but often not considered as much as it should be is the **Cost of Living Allowance or COLA**. This is often set federally as an expected increase in the cost of basic expenses. It changes every year and is something you can find online through federal websites. It is expressed as a percentage and usually is between 1 and 3%. This is an amount that employers should consider for employees that factors in how much the cost of groceries, gas, etc. might increase and how that may affect their quality of life.

Bonuses are always fun to receive and fun to give! I have always found it difficult to administer and recently have created a system that has decreased the mental load of how much to issue and when a bonus should be given. By creating systems with dates and timelines for myself or the person responsible for administering the program, we are able to make sure that we never miss an opportunity to invest in our employees.

When creating a bonus system that is separate from performance raises, consider what behaviours you wish to reward and enhance. I looked at where we spend a lot of money and how we could save that money and share the savings with our employees. For my business, it was in the retention of customers. Acquiring a new customer is always much harder than keeping one we have already found. We have a retention bonus. If the staff achieves a certain retention percentage, the company saves money in marketing and then shares those savings with those who helped make those savings happen.

Another bonus that small businesses often overlook is **years of service awards**. Milestone recognitions that allow you to reward loyalty and longevity. Creating a chart for this will help you ensure that you never miss the chance to celebrate a long-term employee who has brought so much value to the company over the years that they have been working for you.

Employee Benefits are another way to invest in the staff who make your business amazing. Originally, I started offering extra health benefits because I wanted them for my family. Then I saw I was able to use it to show long-time employees my investment in them and their own families. I was able to set up the parameters so that the benefits went to employees who had longevity and commitment to the company.

I was able to extend this further to a retirement savings plan. Using similar criteria, I was able to offer employees plans that were employer-matched. This type of program shows an employee that you care about them in the long run and the future of their lives beyond the company. To me, this is a huge gift to give our staff.

Taking the savings plan one step further, you could even start education savings plans for employees' children. Imagine how loyal an employee might be if you are investing in the future of their children. The possibilities are endless when it comes to showing appreciation and love for those who are helping you move the mission forward every day.

Some of these programs can be time-consuming to administer, but working on systems that will help you to create that lasting value will be worth it. Employees know when they are being cared for and when you are placing importance on their wellbeing, as well as the work they deliver. This is a key component for a staff that is invested in doing their best work for you.

When I was working with Ava on her compensation structure for her large studio in South Dakota, her concern was an employee that was relentless in asking for raises. It was to the point that she feared giving her any positive feedback on a job well done because she was almost instantly met with a request for a raise. As we worked together, we built out a structure that allowed her to no longer have emotional responses to requests but rather be able to look to a chart that would determine if the boxes had been ticked.

Together we worked on charts for:

- Performance raises
- New client enrollment raises
- Retention bonuses
- Years of service bonuses
- Birthday and Christmas gifts
- Certifications and continuing education

We also worked on a plan where the raises and bonuses were given at certain times of the year, allowing for better budgeting and forecasting. Ava has mentioned several times how this structure, which has removed the emotion from it all, has really helped settle her down when it comes time to review and suggest wage increases. It also gives structure around the requests from her staff, so they can understand the cycles and how it affects them.

Compensation

> *You don't get paid for the hour. You get paid for the value you bring to the hour.*
>
> *Jim Rohn*

A way to show your people how important they are to you is the pay structure you have set up for them. We typically see contractors, hourly employees, and salary positions. Contemplate moving that contractor into an hourly employee role. There is security in this opportunity for the contractor, and it may create a better relationship in the long term. Knowing the difference between employees and contractors and how one creates a more sustainable long-term employee relationship could be a valuable asset for your company.

One more opportunity for review would be moving key employees into salary positions. If you have people who are loyal to the cause and indispensable, it may be time to offer them the security of a steady paycheque and the reward of salary and the peace of mind it can bring.

A client of mine, Sean, in California, is in the process of switching his contractors to employees. We worked together to map out the strategy and steps required and uncovered some vital details in this process. I have shared them below to help navigate the process.

1. Be sure to consult an HR company or employment lawyer to ensure you have all the details for the labour laws in your area.
2. You need to ensure that your employment contracts reflect the most current laws and policies that you need to enforce.
3. Check with your accountant to ensure that when you make the switch, it also aligns with your bookkeeping and year-end, or you may trigger extra expenses and headaches.
4. Research if a payroll company may be of benefit to you to help with deductions and submissions. Many of them have time-saving features for time cards and auto-deposit for your employees.
5. Create an education campaign for your employees to understand what will change in their pay and the extra taxes that you collect and submit on their behalf, as well as the taxes the employer matches and submits.
6. Adjust your wage budgets to reflect the new wage amounts so you do not have any surprises at year-end or even monthly.
7. Give yourself time to implement the change. You may need a couple of months to get all the pieces lined up before you can make the change.

Employee Education

Formal education will make you a living; self-education will make you a fortune.

Jim Rohn

One investment that never loses for our company is employee education. By putting some skin in the game and investing in our people to learn how to move the mission forward more efficiently or effectively, they will start to return that learning. It is not uncommon to recover more than 10 times your investment into education. It is always worth the investment.

There is huge value in bringing the experts to you inside the organization rather than sending your people outside of the organization. This is often a more cost-effective solution and has a huge impact on your internal culture that an external event cannot.

You may be thinking, "Sure, but what if I pay for the education and they take it down the street and use it at another workplace?" I agree this is a concern. I have been burned in the past by this too. I have definitely had an employee take thousands of dollars of education down the street and open her own school. However, while she was with me, I grew as a company. My learning now is to invest but also set parameters around it. I have a policy about staff education that the company invests in. It is our right to protect our hard-earned money. Here is an example of what we have in place to protect us at my company:

When termination occurs for any reason:

- *<12 months after completion of the course, program, or activity: employee refunds 100% of the cost.*
- *>12 months but <24 months after completion of the course, program, or activity: employee refunds 50% of the cost.*

If an employee takes me up on paying for education, they understand it is with these parameters tied to it. Or they can choose to pay for it themselves and not worry about the policy we have.

Creating Better Employee Relationships

If you are lucky enough to be someone's employer, then you have a moral obligation to make sure people do look forward to coming to work in the morning.

John Mackey

Using personality inventories helps teams build better communication patterns. I select a new test every year or two to keep it exciting to learn about each other and how you work best together. Learn the love languages of your staff: understand how they like to receive criticism that is constructive, as well as compliments for jobs well done. By knowing this, you can be sure that praise lands the best way it can. Using the results of the five love languages and inventories of skill sets, you will be able to navigate creating a team where everyone is sitting in their sweet spot. You may even uncover skills that you did not know the employee had. Then leverage those superpowers to ensure you are all winning in the workplace.

Use gifts and care packages to highlight celebrations and recognize achievements, or even just to celebrate certain times of the year. Consider using weekly Rockstar recognition awards that are peer-recognized. Help them see and celebrate each other doing exceptional work. This improves company culture in ways that are immeasurable. Be sure you are catching your employees doing things well. Highlight those behaviours you wish to see more of. You don't need to always be correcting to get results.

Look for apprenticeship programs, and create opportunities for your staff to mentor others. This helps them solidify their knowledge by sharing it with someone else and helps to elevate their own feeling of expertise. By cross-training your people, you gain elevated learning across the team and increased competency, as they become seen as an expert by their peers. That is a win around the table for everyone.

Host team-building events to create camaraderie, deepen relationships and improve outcomes with your team. Allow them a chance to get to know each other outside of the office. By creating a culture of care and concern, you will discover they are willing to help each other more when life gets tough. On sick days, they will cover for each other. During life events that take people out of the office, they will pick up dropped tasks and fill in gaps. The team will do this when they are connected and valued. Creating connections within the team is important to longevity and improved results.

Action Item – Hiring Practices

- *Review your onboarding practices and create templates to ensure an employee's first day is always as productive as possible and that you are prepared for them to start work.*

Action Item – Contracts, Handbooks, Job Descriptions

- *Review contracts to ensure you have all the clauses required to execute for all types of scenarios in your industry.*
- *Review handbooks to ensure all policies are in one place for employees to find and read as needed.*
- *Review every position in your company, and ensure each role has a job description and a method and structure to review expectations.*
- *Make sure each description has KRAs and KPIs attached so employees know what success in their role looks like.*

Action Item – Raises and Compensation

- *Pay structure*
- *Bonus structures*
- *COLA*
- *Benefits*
- *Performance bonuses*
- *Service bonuses*
- *Gifts*
- *What other ways can you show your employees how much they matter?*

Action Item – Better Employees

- *Review team-building practices: what can you add to help your team be more cohesive?*
- *Put it in the company calendar so it becomes a priority.*

CHAPTER 11 – CULTURE

---

*If a company has great culture, it can be
the backbone of their success.*

Gary Vaynerchuk

Culture is something that companies believe makes them unique. It is the backbone by which they make decisions and policies. It is the beliefs and the behaviours that surround transactions and business conducted daily. Culture is not there on day one. It develops organically over time through repeated and rewarded behaviours. The traits of the people you hire over time will amplify the culture you are organically developing.

So if we can't have it from day one and we have to grow it over time, where do we start? Peter Drucker famously wrote, "Culture eats strategy for breakfast." This does not mean to suggest that strategy is not important, but a powerful and empowering culture is the faster route to success. So, where do we start to build our company culture?

It starts with how our leader walks the walk and talks the talk. Our leader determines the direction the culture grows. The beliefs that they hold true in the workplace will become what is predominant. If they believe in hard work and long hours, the company will structure itself around the grind. If the leader believes in laughter and the celebration of wins, then the company will focus on the good times that come from the wins.

Culture is a word that we use to define our collective values as an organization. What type of behaviour is prevalent and encouraged?

- Is it a safe place to make mistakes? Can learning happen without threats or fear?
- Is it high-performing? What is the expectation of productivity on a regular day?
- Is it welcoming to new staff or new customers? Can they find their way to feel included and accepted?
- Whatever it takes to get results – no matter the cost? What does that look like over time?
- Is it a team that supports each other and will pitch in to get the job done – even if it is not their role? Focused on the outcome of the company as a whole rather than individual glory?
- How disciplined is the environment? What is the expectation for time management and accountability?
- How is growth or adaptation encouraged or dissuaded?
- What is the mental state of the employees? Eager to take on more, or strained and overworked?

These are just a few ideas around culture foundations that can really drive a culture to go one way or another.

Culture is the lens through which we make decisions, and it is also the way we present ourselves to the outside world. It is the foundation on which we stand. It is how we as a company can imagine our future, the way we tell our stories; it is what we focus on. It is the way we see the world through the eyes of our organization and our potential for impact.

I am often asked as a coach how to change a culture inside of an existing company. My first question is: Has it always been this way? Followed by: When did it change?

Almost always, it is the result of a single employee who was allowed to stay too long and create too much unrest. That always leads back to a leader who let it happen. The short answer to how do I change my company culture? You have to change yourself first.

What Are Your Values

The first step toward change is awareness. If you want to get from where you are to where you want to be, you have to start becoming aware of the choices that lead you away from your desired destination.

Darren Hardy

Darren Hardy has amazing training that walks through your values. In his training, he explains how your values are your compass for choices and behaviour. Just as you might do this activity to determine what is important to you – what do you value personally? – the same activity can be done for your organization. You may discover your personal values are not always in alignment with your organization. You can do a Google search for "value word lists." You will get many results that you can use for the Action Item at the end of this chapter.

The point here is that the values for your company should be stretching toward the goal of your company. The values will shape the decisions and outcomes for the organization. Try and narrow the values down to 7-12 words. These will become part of the guiding "laws" of your organization.

With this narrowed-down values list, you will build the kinds of statements that Mike Michalowicz refers to as "Immutable Laws."

We now have a list of words that we can make into statements that will define our company ethos. The reason we want to have that shorter list of words is that we do not want these statements to lose their power. Rather, we want them to be bold and simple to understand. The basis of our company culture is phrases to make decisions through. It speaks to what we will tolerate and what we will not. It emphasizes what we will focus on and what we will not.

For my company, here were the words that became our value words:

- Responsibility
- Education
- Progress
- Safe
- Self-respect
- Clarity

Immutable Laws

> *Immutable Laws are a blend of ethics, core values and self-assigned law, all wrapped up into one. They are the rules we have defined for ourselves, almost subconsciously, on what is right and what is wrong. What is acceptable and what is not. What makes you happy and what doesn't. They are with you for life and they barely ever change.*
>
> *Mike Michalowicz*

From here, we took those words to build the things we will and will not tolerate as the backbone of who we are and how we make decisions. For fun, we used song titles to dress up the idea and make it memorable to our employees. These "Immutable Laws" are deeply important to us. If we are struggling to make a decision, we come back to if that decision has room inside of these statements. I highly recommend this process outlined in the book *The Pumpkin Plan*, also written by Mike Michalowicz.

DOLLA DOLLA BILLS YO

If there is no $, there is no mission. Without it, our business dies - we treat it with the utmost care and respect by monitoring it through budgets, projections, and goals.

Everyone needs to do their part to earn their wage.

WIND BENEATH MY WINGS

Creating a strong community inside **AND** outside of the studio is important in raising tomorrow's leaders. By teaching life skills and connecting with our community, we exemplify leadership and stewardship.

NO LIMITS

Pushing the limits on industry norms is a **GOOD** thing. Healthy things **GROW**. Just as we expect the business to grow, we expect staff to grow too. In order to shake it up, we expect innovation and excellence through professional development. We chase blue sky - the only limits are the ones you place on yourself!

SAFE AND SOUND

We strive to keep a safe learning environment for our students by teaching proper technique, background checking our teachers and volunteers, and equipping our staff with First Aid.

BUT it's also a safe place for staff; we encourage you to grow, and to learn from mistakes - and from each other.

HERO TO ZERO

No one person is required to take heroic measures to take their tasks, and no one is expected to pour from an empty cup - we want you to pour from your **OVERFLOW**. To take care of others, and be awesome team players, we must first take care of ourselves.

BYE BYE BYE

Being a jerk is not acceptable; we won't accept jerks as clients, vendors, or employees. We will never be jerks. Life is too short. Jerks not allowed.

Culture Amplified

Don't tell them what you're going to do – that's vision. Do what you are going to do – that's culture.

John C. Maxwell

As our company culture grows and the values of our staff begin to be amplified, there are many benefits that start to unfold. Companies with strong cultures can boast a lot about the rewards of a positive culture. Over time, I have collected these ideas about culture from various conferences and coaches. I showed you how we had grown before with our Mission and Vision Statements, and this is the same idea. It has evolved over time through collecting ideas and steady implementation.

Higher Productivity Rate: Having happier people means they get more done and are happy to do it.
Increased Job Satisfaction: When you enjoy where you spend a lot of your time, you get excited to go and be successful there.
Higher Employee Retention: Happier people will stay with their employer longer. Longer careers mean better results for a company that is not retraining all the time.
Overall Employee Wellness: Happier people need less time off to manage their stress. They get sick less often, and they have a better overall outlook.
Attracting Potential Recruits: The word of a good employer moves fast. People want to work for a company that matches their own values, a place that will reward their hard work and skill sets.
Lower Stress Environment: When you enjoy your workplace, your stress level is reduced. Lower stress means better health, wellness, and productivity.
Happy Employees: People will always do more than expected when they are appreciated. Happy employees know they are valued and are willing to go the extra mile for the mission.

Culture Levers

Companies have so many creative levers to pull in order to improve or redirect company culture as it grows. We continue to influence the culture every day by who we allow contact with our culture and how they interact.

The first lever we can pull is **staff hiring**. We want to hire people who inherently fit our values. If the boss values the grind and you hire someone who values balance and free time – you may have a clash of values that puts pressure on everyone. Instead, think about the types of questions in an interview that could help you find out if they have a similar value structure.

Some questions that we can include in our hiring process could be:

- What are some of your career goals?
- What do you know about us, and what value do you bring to our team?
- What are your three top qualities?
- What motivates you?
- What are your goals for working with us?
- Why do you want this job?

The second lever is **staff onboarding**. How we onboard someone matters. Those first few days on the job will set the tone for values and expectations for years to come.

I know you will find this story to be familiar. Sam gets hired for a new job, and he is excited for the first day. He shows up with enthusiasm and is ready to work, but no one is expecting him, and the people he met through the interview process are nowhere to be found. There is no work desk set up, no place to sit or start working, and he doesn't have a company email or phone number. Then begins a long uncomfortable morning of losing interest in the new position, of no productivity, and of awkward conversation about the person who Sam replaced. Then Sam starts to realize he will have to train himself, and the success rate for his new job just dropped by 50%. Soon Sam will move on to another workplace where he feels valued and appreciated. The company will wonder how it didn't work out when he seemed like a great fit.

To change this scenario to match more positive values, Sam could have received a communication saying, "We are excited to meet you tomorrow at 9:00 a.m. Your contact will be Jane Smith. She will give you a tour, introduce you to the team, and get you settled in your workspace. Your training partner will be John, and he will start your training and get you going on your first project. The team meeting is at 1:00 p.m., where we will give you a big welcome to the team!"

Which scenario shows a culture you wish to work in?

When you hire new people: Are you ready for them to be there that day? Do you value productivity, but the first day they don't have a workspace or any work to do? Do you value processes, but you do not have training set up for them to be successful right away? Do you value respect in the workplace, but their first encounters are gossip and poor behaviour from others?

Management is another lever to pull. How is management engaging with the rest of the company? Does the manager recast the vision continuously, and do they show it by example?

I am sure we have all heard stories about the type of manager who shows up to yell at his employees to get the job done and not bother him until it is complete, then disappears behind his office door. Then the employees, disheartened and grumbling, do the work, all the while dreaming of getting "out of this place for good."

In a more positive-culture company, you might see that manager sit down with the team and say, "Alright, we have a huge project and a looming deadline. How shall we tackle this?" Then using his team's skills and talents, he builds a plan where everyone lifts the weight to get it done. Those employees talk about how they love the benefits of a team and feel seen and fulfilled by the management of the company.

How does your management team harness the power and skills of the employees you hire? Do they tell employees they care about their well-being and then demand long hours to get a project done? Does management roll up their sleeves to help when needed, or do they just get mad about missed deadlines and offer little support? Do they talk about "team" and then close the door rather than be on the team? You need to be sure the management team is recasting the culture vision every day in their actions and interactions with the employees.

When it is time to **offboard a staff person,** how is it done? Is there a process that is repeatable and respectful, regardless of the reasons for the employee leaving?

Jack needs to be let go. He has missed too many deadlines and ruffled too many feathers. He is no longer helping the team. Everyone has known for months that he needs to go. He makes everyone uncomfortable with his distasteful jokes and poor choices for conversation. He has spent weeks talking about everyone in the company and how bad they are at their job and how he is the only one who gets anything done. Three people have already quit rather than continue to work with him.

In a company with a strong positive culture, Jack started to miss deadlines and had a few conversations that made people uncomfortable with his tone and topic choice. Jack was called in to talk to his manager, who asked him, "You are not yourself lately. When can I expect you to be back on your game?" Jack explained that he had some personal life pressures that had followed him to work recently and that he thought he might need to move jobs to manage. He and his manager agreed he should take the opportunity and that they could wish him well in his new endeavour. The manager asked him to make things right with his peers on the way out. Jack agreed to do so.

When there is trouble on your team, do you ignore it or get right after it? Do the other employees see a respectful process? Do you actually keep private details private, or is it talked about in their absence? How is it handled by management, and what are other employees asked to respond with or communicate when asked? This is another opportunity to imprint your culture. Everyone sits up a little straighter when staff leave the team, regardless of the reason they leave. Use this time to reinforce your values to those who stay.

We can also affect culture by the customers we choose. While it would be wonderful to think that every person out there is a potential customer, the truth is that we know that we do not want to serve everyone. Not every person can be our customer. We have to be specific about who we are trying to serve and how we reach them. So how does the customer affect our culture?

Customer onboarding is one way that we can ensure we have the right people for our company to serve. The way our customer learns to interact with us helps us ensure we can be successful serving them. If you are selling questions and support anytime but only answer the phone from 9 a.m. to 5 p.m., you may pick up customers who give you a hard time when they can't get support at midnight. If you teach them the proper channels to get the help they need and the expectations around that service, you could develop a long-lasting relationship.

Sally just became a customer. She is demanding and, within her first two interactions, has made the cashier cry and requested to speak to the manager. She is now telling the manager how she wants to do business, and it "better be my way." The manager has told the cashier that she better find a way to make it work with the customer regardless of how she is being treated. Sally comes in all the time, and now the cashier dreads coming to work. The cashier is looking for a new job that doesn't feel so unsafe.

Customer offboarding is another way you instill your values in your team. Do you say you won't tolerate the poor treatment of your staff and then continually send them into situations where clients do not treat them well? Do you have a system for when a customer is just no longer a fit? Do you stand up for the treatment of your staff? Do you have the courage to tell a customer when you are not the best fit for their needs? Are you consistent in this message? How do you rally the troops in the wake of a lost customer? This is another opportunity to drive home what your core values are and encourage the culture to grow in adversity.

Sally has just walked into the salesroom for a company with positive culture. She doesn't like the price and has already had a run-in with the cashier. The manager overhears the commotion and steps into the conversation to provide the cashier support in this difficult transaction. After hearing the customers' concerns, the manager decides that Sally is not quite the type of customer they want to serve, as she doesn't seem to have respect for the policies and processes in place. The manager respectfully suggests that another store might be able to fill her needs. When Sally leaves, the manager affirms that the cashier did well and affirms the decisions made. They may do training on an item or two about what they learned from the interaction with Sally, but the cashier continues their shift knowing that the company means it when they say they are only serving customers who have respectful interactions.

The last lever I will discuss here is **marketing**. What does your internal and external marketing do to convey your values? Are you saying you value family-friendliness and then have questionable images? Do you say you are for everyone and then have trouble serving an inclusive market? Does your internal message match the external message? Do you show happy, healthy images, but when people visit your store, they see tired and grumpy employees struggling through their day?

Be sure to use images that match the experience. People want to feel like they recognize the feelings or images they associate with your business when they visit. Be sure to use real images of your location and not stock photos that portray something different from what is experienced if they actually show up. Be authentic, and your customers will expect the experience you have set out through the marketing.

Culture is the way we celebrate our employees and customers. It is how we remember our company history. It is how we reach the goals we set and create meaningful employment.

Culture is driven by everyday decisions on what you choose to say yes to and how you choose to execute it. Culture is a living, breathing, and changing force of energy inside your company, and you have to spend time weeding it, nurturing it, and growing it. It needs constant care and attention to detail. You cannot leave it to become overgrown or unmanageable, or it can sink the whole vision. Every person you hire is responsible for its growth or decline. This is why it is so necessary to be clear on who you are and what you will tolerate. It is challenged with every hire and interaction inside your company every day.

Action Item – Values

Do a Google search for "value word lists." Using the list you found, read through it and circle the words that are important to you. It could be things like:

- *Loyalty*
- *Competence*
- *Discretion*
- *Practicality*
- *Recognition*
- *Synergy*
- *Teamwork*
- *Winning*

Try and narrow the values down to 7-12 words.
These will become part of your guiding "laws of your organization."

Action Item – Immutable laws

Now take those words and build your "Laws" for your company. By asking your employees to help, you can turn this into a team-build.

Action Item – Culture Levers

Review all the levers we discussed, and see which ones you can pull to amplify the culture you wish to see:

- *Staff hiring*
- *Staff onboarding*
- *Management*
- *Offboarding*
- *Customer onboarding*
- *Customer offboarding*
- *Marketing*

CHAPTER 12 – SYSTEM EXPANSION

Management works in the system; leadership works on the system.

Stephen Covey

Once our business has been up and running for several months, maybe even years, we will start to see that there may be a better way. One that we couldn't afford at start-up but is now available to us. Or now that we have the skill set, we can see there are better ways to track and manage our business more efficiently. This type of growth can only be found after we have tested our process and systems to see where improvements can and need to be made.

Why Automate

The first rule of any technology used in a business is that automation applied to an efficient operation will magnify the efficiency. The second is that automation applied to an inefficient operation will magnify the inefficiency.

Bill Gates

Automating tasks may have a heavy front-load effort, but it is all about time balance. For example, it will take 20 hours of time investment to set up the new payroll program. The new program will allow us to save 10 hours every two weeks when we run payroll, but we just can't seem to justify the time investment at the start – our schedule is just too busy; we are, after all, running a business, and we have a lot of tasks to do.

Put another way: if we find 20 hours this week to set up that program, we can save 260 hours annually. Yes, we might be busy, but if we can spend 20 hours to save 260 hours – that is an efficiency worth looking into. If we looked at many of our larger projects with this mindset, it would be really easy to clear the calendar and make time for this setup. This is a clear, easy win for our time and the company.

A great example of this was when my client Barbra needed to implement a new payroll system. She had spent several months talking about how she was going to get to it, but she could never set aside the time and just sit down and do the work. Each month, she spent several hours reviewing errors and manually cutting cheques and making corrections, all the while getting more and more frustrated with her staff and their timesheet errors. When I finally gave her some tough love and put my foot down that she must get it done before the next payroll, she grumbled and agreed it was more than time to get the project done. After all that procrastination, it took her half the time she thought it would to implement and get it set up. Now she enjoys that it takes her less than three hours to manage her monthly payroll, and there are only 5% of the errors she used to have to work through previously. When you ask her about it today, she sheepishly agrees that she spent much more time complaining about it than it took to get it implemented and that she is much happier with less time going into the task each month.

So why automate? What makes automation so important, especially for the small business owner? Automation is a key element in winning back your time, sanity, and money! Here are a few benefits to automation:

- Free up valuable time by setting and forgetting
- Save staff hours
- Create consistency in sales and onboarding experience
- Shorten buying period
- Outsource tasks to stay in your zone of genius

Automation in Sales

There are a few areas that are easy pickings for automation. One of those is sales. In sales, we can automate:

- Lead generation
- Trials/consults
- Social media posts

Automating Leads

To automate leads, there are several approaches. Most of us start off with a system that has little to no tracking. We might have a notebook or scrap paper where we write down some details, but we do not track enough information for statistics, just enough to serve the customer.

After enough missed sales opportunities and money slipping through our fingers, we may start a spreadsheet that tracks the name, details of the sale, and contact information. We can start to see some trends in this data, but not every customer is on the sheet and we still don't track everything coming in because the other salespeople sometimes forget, or they don't see how valuable this information could be, so it is not important to them.

Finally, we get to the place where we realize this could be automated. The automation removes the need for our staff to enter it or not; it removes the emotion they have around the importance to them. We get to collect everything we need to know about who our customer base is and narrow our focus to really serve what they are looking for.

Some of the tools we use to automate in my business are:

- Landing pages
- Customer journey tracking
- E-commerce marketing management

Landing Pages

> *Landing pages need to be appealing, but most of all, they need to convert.*
>
> *Russell Brunson*

Landing page builders and management software are so important for our advertising online. These programs help us track traffic from ads, so we know which ones are performing well and which ones we need to scrap or tweak for better performance. These tools allow us to create a page, which our ad leads to, that encourages the customer to leave their details to gain access to a coupon or the product. When the customer leaves their information for us, we get data about the buyer: what they wanted, what time they shopped for it, how popular that ad was, who they were, etc. We can design our page to capture the information that helps us serve that client better.

The key to a great landing page is an effective offer or call to action. Make sure there is only one so as not to confuse our customers. The ad they click on should also lead them to a landing page that "feels" the same as the ad. Don't confuse the customer by using different graphics or language from the ad to the landing page. It should be clear what the next step is for the customer.

Some examples of landing page software include Leadpages or Hubspot.

Customer Journey Tracking

Focusing on the customer makes a company more resilient.

Jeff Bezos

This tool has been really important for our company's growth and excellence in service delivery. We mapped out what we want the customer journey to be like when they are with us, all the touchpoints and opportunities to cross-sell and upsell. The purpose of this is to understand that no matter when a customer onboards with us, they will have the same experience as another customer. This starts to create consistent experiences and strengthens our customer base.

We map things like follow-up phone calls, surveys, newsletters, onboarding steps, birthday cards, and one-on-one meetings to discuss goals and needs, so we know what the expectations are. The program we use allows us to see when they joined us, what experiences they have had so far, and what we still need to do to ensure they have a great experience the way we want all customers to have.

We also use this software to help us navigate processes like complaints. We are able to track what the issue was, how it was solved, and if the solution was workable. We check back a few weeks later to ensure that they are still happy with the solution. An example of this is a change in class time to accommodate a better schedule. In some cases, when we call back to make sure the solution did what they hoped, they are happy to hear from us and would like to return to the original time. This is a huge win in customer service. In the majority of these instances, they did not want to bother us again but are glad we contacted them.

We can use it to track accounts receivable or payment plans. The program will provide us with the check-in points to make sure that we are collecting payments and keeping clients with payment plans on track. This has been really helpful for identifying repeat offenders or clients that may not be our ideal customer. It has saved hours of tracking down communication or wondering if we sent the right communication to be able to take the next step in this account. Sometimes, in an effort to provide above-and-beyond service, we end up with several accounts that do not follow the normal pattern, and it is easy to forget when to follow up with which customer. With this system in place, we rarely have a customer fall through the cracks, and that saves us staff time chasing overdue accounts.

E-commerce Marketing Management

If you do build a great experience, customers tell each other about that. Word of mouth is very powerful.

Jeff Bezos

Our e-commerce marketing management program helps us keep track of all our leads and clients, and create a variety of client pools: clients who are interested in certain products, people who interacted with a certain web page, or leads that have not yet purchased. We can use these programs to sort our leads and customers in endless ways. Then we can take all those sorting features and use them to advertise our products and services. We can design advertising campaigns or consumer education programs that can then be shared with the contacts in our list.

These programs also provide us with data about how they interact with our campaigns. Things like open rates and click-throughs, and the number of opens and unsubscribes. Don't be worried about those unsubscribes; they keep our list clean and current. It means that people who stay subscribed may not be ready to buy today, but they may in the future. Those are great leads to keep in our funnel.

In today's online marketing world, a program like this can save you many hours of sorting clients and track things we cannot do on paper. Some e-commerce management programs are: Get Drip and Mail Chimp.

Automating Trials or Consults

In today's marketing, we will often see free trials or free consult appointments. The reason this is so prevalent is that the opportunity for a consumer to experience the service before buying increases the longevity of a customer and shortens the buying process. By allowing them to experience the service or product free of charge, we can increase the consumer confidence that this is the right thing for them to buy, and they can feel good buying it.

The problem is that the back-and-forth and time investment to get a consumer to the free trial or consult appointment can often cost hours of time in communication. Many companies like to limit the free trials of consults they offer so they can ensure they have time dedicated to the needs of paying customers as well.

We may have started out just pencilling in these trials by phone or email as they came in, but at some point, the pencil in the agenda becomes too time-consuming and frustrating for a customer who really just wants to book. The back-and-forth can sometimes be a turnoff as they envision that every time they need an appointment, this will be the case. They can move on to the next business that seems easier to deal with.

We may have tried a solution where the times were set, but they still had to get a manual confirmation in order to attend. That means there is still some back-and-forth to confirm the appointment time. This is still not as smooth as today's buyers expect it to be.

The best solution and the one that is worth the research and setup is an automated system that shows the customer what time slots are available in an online calendar or similar format. The consumer can choose the appointment time that best suits them, and they receive an automated email reply confirming the time.

This requires some back-end setup and pre-scripted emails giving all the information they need to make the most of their trial consult. In some cases, the process can invite the consumer to also provide some detail prior to the meeting to ensure the time is well spent together. This system saves everyone time and frustration and shows your consumer right from the start that you have attention to detail and that you care about the experience. The pre-scripted emails can start to share your mission, your why, the reason why you are different from your competitors, and why they can feel good about a purchase with you. Examples of automated scheduling are Calendly and Acuity.

Automating Social Media

Social media marketing is about creating content that brings your audience together as a community and inspiring authentic conversations while increasing your brand's awareness.

Krystal Wu

Social media is the great beast of our day. Many people will tell you it is free, but we have already discussed that time is the one resource we cannot get back. Once we spend it, it is gone. Social media is one of those business needs that can suck up more time than you know, and it does cost—it may not always be advertising dollars, but it takes our time and often pulls us off task for way longer than anticipated.

We may have started off advertising our business on our personal page. Every time we go to make a business post, we end up scrolling to see what is going on out there. More time sucked away from our schedule. Maybe at some point, we decide to make a business page to create some more credibility, but it takes time to post every day and make sure that we have a presence and some followers. Every time we crack open that program, we are tempted to scroll and see what else is out there.

By automating your social media, you will see a few things happen:

- You will save time.
- You will become more efficient.
- Your messaging will become more effective.
- Your brand will be stronger and more cohesive.

By batching and automated posting, we will start to spend less time on social media in general. In our schedule, we can start to block out time to create a week or a month's worth of posts in one sitting. By doing it all at once, we will start to be able to shape the narrative better and create consistent language and messaging. We can start to see a plan come together for how and why we post what we post. We can create a better balance of giving and asking.

The best part is that after creating all that content, we can schedule it, so we do not have to go into our social media accounts every day to make the posts. This will save hours. Hours of time thinking up what to say tomorrow, unintended scrolling, and more. By working this way in batches and using a scheduled posting program, we will be able to be efficient with the time we spend on social media. We may even see that it gets better results because it is planned and intentional.

These programs will also capture data. Which posts were engaging, and which ones missed the mark? They can tell us click-throughs and what type of person clicked. Are we attracting females or males, age bracket, and in some cases, demographics such as parents of young kids, toddlers, or teens. We can learn about what their interests are or target people who have certain interests. These programs can also help us with retargeting and more. Once we get out of the time-sucking part of social media, we can start to use the time for better-intentioned outcomes.

Automation in HR

---

*Human resources are the most valuable
assets the world has. They are all needed
desperately.*

Eleanor Roosevelt

Automation in our human resources and staffing components will also begin to save us time. I can't tell you how many times I have been at work and the employee files were locked up at home, or vice versa, and I didn't have the tools I needed to do the next task. Paper copies of things like manuals and handbooks are constantly out of date and needing to be reprinted and refreshed. Imagine having all our staff onboarding and pieces of training readily available for new hires and retraining at our fingertips for current staff!

There are several things to automate in HR:

- Employee files
- Training and certifications
- Payroll
- Hiring
- Onboarding and offboarding

Employee files being automated has saved me hundreds of hours. Having contracts with digital signatures and a program that keeps track of what paperwork is outstanding or due to be signed again have allowed me to keep everything current and onside of employment standards. It has been a huge time saver to be able to reissue paperwork easily with the click of a button right to that employee's email and have them sign it and automatically upload to their employee folder, where we can both look at it whenever either of us needs to. No more printing contracts and preparing envelopes with several documents, and then remembering to chase down the unfinished paperwork.

Several times before we automated this, employees would neglect to bring paperwork back in, and their files would be out of date. This becomes a problem if we ever need to begin corrective action. We have to get everything updated first, then go about the corrective action.

Training and certifications is another area where we can save immense time in automation. By having a program where we can set the expiry of current certifications and set up recurring training, we can have the program deliver messages to the staff to let them know when they need to start making time for the course in their schedule. It also allows the staff to see their history and next steps.

Another way we have been able to save time on training staff has been to record mandatory meetings where important long-term information is given, or record a video of a new procedure for a department. These recordings then become part of the onboarding or reboarding when employees have spent time with the company and may need refresher training. We can email the video link out with a due date and ensure everyone is up to date with the procedure.

This has been a huge time saver when new staff onboard, we have a library of training videos on culture, cleaning, expectations, and more. They are able to watch these training as part of their onboarding, and because they are videos, there is less strain on the person who is responsible for training. They can then be available to answer questions or review, rather than going through the same education for each person who comes through. Programs that can help you manage: Simple CPR and BambooHR.

Automating payroll has also been a huge time saver. Going from paper timesheets that sometimes get turned in and sometimes don't. Chasing staff for hours and invoicing for payment is such a huge waste of time and so frustrating. When I sit down to do payroll, I want to be able to accomplish the task in the time I have allotted for it. I had rules around filling it in every time you work and not leaving it to the end of the pay period and then writing it all in. But *every* time, someone was delinquent in getting their hours in properly and on time. Then all the calculations for statutory holidays and vacation pay, and the list goes on. If this is not your favourite part of the business and it is not your super-power, – hire it out and/or automate it! Trust me, you will get hours back every month to spend on the things that really need your attention.

Finally, I had enough, and we went to an automated payroll system. You had to enter your hours into the system by a certain time, or it locked you out, and you could not make additions or adjustments to that pay period. That saved me the time of hunting down those who were delinquent. It wasn't me not letting you in. It was the way the system worked. It helped me to not have to chase or explain it anymore – it just was.

We still had issues with people forgetting and making work for me to fix it for the next pay period. To solve that, I went to the next level – a thumbprint scanner. You have to "thumb in or out" at the start and end of each shift, or you just don't get paid. Period. It has to be real-time, and you cannot adjust it at the employee level. They have to be willing to come to me and say, "Sorry, I missed doing this part of my job" – *every time they forget*. This has been the best automation so far. While the machine cost me a bit to implement, I can say the savings in just two pay periods have more than covered the cost of the equipment. You would be surprised how easy it is for employees to charge for hours that were not real working hours. 15 min here and there adds up, and it is company theft – theft of payroll.

Automating hiring has also been a huge time saver. The program that we use to manage employee files also helps manage the hiring process. This means it tracks candidates and where they are in our hiring funnel. Have they applied before? How far did they go? Who has interviewed them and what type of interview did they do? Comments as they go through the funnel can be left for the next person who interacts with them. The best part is that because it is the same system with the click of a button, they have an employee file and can be onboarded easily if they are a successful candidate. We no longer wonder if we have seen the resume before, or is this a new person? Who has met with them? What questions have they already been asked?

Automating the hiring process has saved us tens of thousands of dollars. Bad hires are expensive. Having this tool helps us ensure the whole hiring process is consistent and followed. It has saved us bad hires and poor training expenses.

By extension, we have also been able to **automate the onboarding process**. We have been able to template everything that needs to happen for every employee when they join the team, as well as things that may be specific to their role. We used to realize they had no email only after they didn't reply to communications, or shoot! No employee jacket ready! Or no key for the door on hand when they started. The list of how terrible hiring can sometimes be. Now we have an accurate list of everything they need and when they need it by. We also have a list of things we need from them and when we need the information from them. It is clearly laid out and funnels out as soon as they are hired. The process is so smooth, and we are really proud of it.

By extension, we have also **automated offboarding**. There are times when it is time to part ways, and having the offboarding process clearly outlined removes the emotion that can sometimes accompany an employee exiting. It allows us to ensure the security of proprietary information, the building, and the employee's privacy. Again, it is a list of tasks that are templated, and when it is executed, we know exactly which step belongs to which person and how fast it needs to be completed. Program examples are Payworks, Ceridian, and Bamboo HR.

Hit-by-a-Bus Plan

Sometimes it's good to miss a bus. It might be the wrong bus.

Steve Guttenberg

Automating Tasks and the Operations Manual

Business owners are the worst offenders for having the entire business manually in their brains and not taking the time to get it on paper. I call this process of getting all the details out where they can benefit the staff and be accessible: writing your "Hit-by-a-Bus Plan."

The thing about a "Hit-by–a-Bus Plan" is that it is not **if** you will ever need it; it is **when**. As my mentor, Darren Hardy, says, "Shiitake will happen." You need to plan for that day when you will not be able to be in your business. You need to set your team up for success in your absence. You have to plan for everything to continue along, no matter what happens.

We have spent the better part of four years getting our operations manual and all of our tasks out of everyone's heads and into a format that can be used. It has been so freeing to not wonder what I forgot and just know that my daily calendar will tell me what needs to get done next. It frees my mind to be able to dream, plan, and be visionary when I am not bogged down with the details of everyday life.

Task-Management Automation

> *Let our advance worrying become advance thinking and planning.*
>
> *Winston Churchill*

We chose a task-management software program that allows us to break things down by section of our company, such as recitals, parties, costumes, event days, and so forth. Make no mistake: this is a huge initiative and takes an immense amount of work, but it is absolutely vital that you get this done. It started with a four-day off-site and then rolled into everyday management of the content that lives in this program.

We sat down with the leadership team and said, "Tell me the categories of this company that you intersect with." They had sticky notes and wrote down everything they could think of that they did in that section of the company. We took all those notes and added to them the time of year and how often it recurs, and then we arranged them on the wall into sections. Then each section was entered into our task-management system with a person who is responsible, a due date, and how often that task recurs. This took an immense amount of work.

From here, we then said if our task-management software is WHAT NEEDS TO GET DONE, then we also need a tool that records HOW TO DO IT. It is not enough to only know what needs to get done; we also have to record how it gets done. We have to assume there will be a time when the person who always does it is not available to do the task. Whether they are out sick or have left the company, there needs to be a built-in mechanism for us to be able to get that task done even if they are not there to do it.

Operations Manual Automation

Most people treat the office manual the way they treat a software manual. They never look at it.

James Levine

For us, we decided we were not going to build a stale, dusty book that sits on a shelf, completely out of date, and no one even knows what is in it. We decided we would build an online, living document in a searchable and editable format. This was a huge initiative for our company and one that has been incredible. We took those sticky notes that were laid out in the previous task automation and said, "Now for all the things you are responsible for, you have to write instructions that someone who does not do your job could follow if they needed to."

We decided on a format that each page would have so that it would be easy to find the details and understand the information on the pages. The program we chose allowed us to embed videos of screen shares, screenshots for reference, and links to documents that are required for the task. By having everything you need built out in the document, it became an all-inclusive business brain for everything we do at the company. Below is an example of the page layout. This was adapted from Dave Crenshaw's training on the myth of multitasking. Program example: Google Site.

Every page is laid out the same way. The who, what, and why for every task is outlined. My favourite part of this is that we can see who created it and when. This helps us determine if the process is obsolete or current. Every person who has created a page has to have another person test the instructions to see if there is enough information to get the task completed.

Once that is the case, and the task can be completed by someone else, the task in our management software also gets a link to the instructions for that task. Now when someone else has to do that task, they are one click away from the instructions. There are no more excuses for something to get missed or be done incorrectly.

The operations manual is online and available to employees. We can search tasks, we can edit them if they have changed, and we can add new information and delete old information. This is not printed; it is a living document that is changing daily in our company. No more massive, outdated books printed and gathering dust.

Recently we have taken this format one step further and created an information center for our business, where the home page has links to all the programs you need to do your job effectively. Links to our client database, social media, appointment booking, financial software, the bank—anything that is a frequently used site, we have an information console. I can just sit at my desk and open that home page, and I have everything I need. No more searching for URLs or passwords. Everything is efficiently in one place, waiting for employees to be effective in their workdays.

When we dive into the world of automation, we start to see how we can gain our time back, make our company run more efficiently, and gain more productivity from all our people. Who doesn't want that?

Action Item – Audit Your Automations

- *What can you automate in your sales process?*
- *What can you automate in your leads process?*
- *What can you automate in your landing pages process?*
- *What can you automate in your customer journey tracking process?*
- *What can you automate in your e-commerce process?*
- *What can you automate in your trials or consults process?*
- *What can you automate in your social media process?*
- *What can you automate in your HR process?*

Action Item – Task Management

Is there an opportunity for you to automate the tasks that run your business daily?

Start mapping the steps you need to take to get this project done.

Action Item – Operations Manual

Is there an opportunity for you to automate your operations manual?

Start mapping the steps you need to take to get this project done.

CHAPTER 13 – WORLDWIDE PIVOTS

Starting is not most people's problem, staying, continuing and finishing is.

Darren Hardy

The biggest question that we as business owners have heading into the next decades of business is how to adapt to be better stewards of our client's needs and the communities we serve and live in. It is our responsibility to look around us and leave the world better than how we came into it. How can your business make a change for the better? What practices or policies do you need to change or embrace? Where can you lead to make a better change? How can you inspire your team to make a positive contribution to the community beyond your four walls?

Changing World in Children's Education

Anyone who does anything to help a child in his life is a hero to me.

Fred Rogers

Over the past few years, we have seen more children's educators in the news in a variety of youth sport and activities for the wrong reasons: educators who have taken advantage of the vulnerable children in their care and abused their position of authority and the duty of care they had accepted. My staff and I saw this as a place where we could make a change for our industry and start to set the bar higher for ourselves.

We set out to work with an organization called Youth Protection Advocates in Dance (YPAD). This group gave us words to put to the duty of care under which we had been operating for years. It gave us a banner to fly around the considerations and great care we took to ensure we were creating safe spaces for our children, and for our teens to safely grow into themselves without fear or judgment. The YPAD certification was a way that we were able to stand out in a crowded market and show that we were family-friendly and educated on safe spaces for kids to train with their whole and complete safety in mind.

> *Be more concerned with your character than your reputation, because your character is what you really are, while your reputation is merely what others think you are.*
>
> *John Wooden*

Our staff agreed to put the child before the activity. We learned ways to communicate with parents about injuries and concerns that we could see in our students and to follow through for their health's sake. We were already careful about music and costumes and ensuring we were selective of the messaging and image our students portrayed. This training allowed us to go further and empower our students to stand up and say, "This music is not appropriate for me," or, "This costume is not necessary," when they went out to the larger arts community. I can tell you that those were very proud moments for us as educators. They started to hold other industry professionals to account when we travelled. They did it respectfully and confidently. "Let kids be kids" and "Is this necessary to teach me the performance arts?"

were the messages we carried that our students, now empowered, would echo.

Our staff took deeper training on mandated reporting and identifying students in need. They were empowered to say something when things weren't quite right. We are proud of the safe spaces in our community, and we know that we have actually saved lives. Students who felt they had nowhere else have come to us. Kids who just couldn't find space at school found space with us. Parents have told me many times over the years that their child would not still be with us, that the only reason they are still here is because of a special teacher relationship we gave space to. If we hadn't been who we are for them, they would have taken their own lives. That is a responsibility that we do not take lightly, and we know there will be many more students to come who will need us just as much. We will be ready, arms open, safe space prepared.

YPAD training allowed us to require our staff to be background-checked. Most children's activities do not require this, but almost every parent assumes their instructor is. We set out to reach a higher standard. We also have every staff person certified in first aid and CPR. Both of these are now a requirement to work for us, and everyone gets recertified.

Emergency Preparedness

There's no harm in hoping for the best as long as you're prepared for the worst.

Stephen King

I was startled to find that decidedly few children's activities that happen outside of traditional school buildings have emergency plans. When we look at active aggressors, bomb threats, or even just fires – sadly few businesses have plans other than "This is the way out of the building." I set out to create a plan for us for every scenario. We built out plans for active aggressors and shooters, lockdowns, shelter in place, evacuate and then shelter, and everything in between. We built all these plans out for our building and classrooms, people in the lobbies, and staff. We worked with a local security company to ensure that we had covered the issues that could potentially come up. Every room in the building was equipped with a bucket of emergency supplies and cheat-sheet instructions so the staff could execute no matter the situation. We have annual training on this. Many youth activities do not, and it's quite upsetting, given today's climate and the frequency of terrible disasters.

Once we had created all these plans for our building, we turned our eyes to the places our students visit in the community and how we can prepare for the unthinkable in the world at large. We built out plans for the theatres and venues, parade routes, and trade shows we visit. How can we keep kids safe in the event of an emergency? How do we keep kids safe under YPAD protocols in unfamiliar territory like dressing rooms and open-to-public venues? We created portable emergency kits that travel with us to the performances we go to. We solved for safety concerns ahead of time by creating questions we ask vendors we do business with to help us create safer spaces. In return, they are making better spaces for the next groups that come through, and we are happy to see the community stepping into knowing better and doing better.

We are proud to be leading the standard in our community in such a positive way.

And Then COVID-19 Happened

In Covid times, businesses have been asked to pivot, pivot again, and rearrange one more time. It has asked businesses to redefine themselves, restructure, and invent new ways of delivering products and services in order to survive. It has tested all systems and teams longer and more thoroughly than we ever believed possible by a market trend or an external force on our businesses.

Disruption-Proof Your Business – Pandemic or Recession

I was struck by the work these organizations are doing and while everyone's priority right now is to stay safer at home, I know there are many of us looking for ways to help.

Oprah Winfrey

Let's talk about having a growth mindset during a pandemic. I think there are some questions that leaders need to ask in order to ensure that their teams are moving forward in a productive manner in spite of strenuous circumstances. Nothing is the same. We have to close the door on how we've done business before because it's dramatically irrelevant.

Everything has changed.

We need to act fast. Changes we are experiencing are happening rapidly, and we have to act in equal measure or risk falling behind. We also need to be the solution because the market has changed and customer needs have changed. We have the opportunity to be a hero. A hero is an ordinary person who takes **action** when put into an extraordinary situation. A hero is nothing more than this.

A growth mindset in this situation is key. During the pandemic, you have seen many business owners take a knee: "It is hard work, it's too difficult to change to suit the market, I don't want to change, someone should rescue my business, that costs money to do." The list goes on with whining and "Woe is me, I don't want to do the work." The truth is you don't want to waste a **good pandemic!** The opportunities the problems of a pandemic provide are too good for a true entrepreneur to waste! There is a huge opportunity for you to grab on to in this new market.

So how do we get a growth mindset? How do we harness the potential? How do we make sure we do not waste the opportunity to lead through a global economic crisis? Below, I have assembled some questions that my mentor shared with me early in the pandemic. These questions allowed my business to pivot quickly, and never once did we take a knee. I was able to lead strongly and effectively for the duration of extended lockdowns and economic challenges that came with consumer fatigue and loss of consumer confidence.

Reinvention

When things are bad, it's the best time to reinvent yourself.

George Lopez

The first question to ask is: "What can I deconstruct and/or reinvent?" This is called the Madonna effect. In the 1980s, it looked like the artist known as Madonna would have 15 minutes of fame. Three decades later, after constant reinvention, her sixth world tour in 2004 was aptly titled *Reinvention*. So ask:

1. What are you best at delivering?
2. Even in a pandemic, what has not changed?
3. What would your business look like if you started from scratch right now?

Then get after the task of acting on the answers to those questions. Speed is key. Show your customers that you are capable of ensuring you can adapt and make their concerns part of your response.

Key Skill Sets

How else can key skill sets be used? Products or services sold also have amazing people with unique skill sets and talents behind them. There may even be a source of exponential growth if applied to a new set of problems.

1. What are the key skills of your business?
2. Are there more key skills inside different departments within the business?
3. Where can those skills be redeployed?

Start on this task sooner than a pandemic: start now. What skills exist on your team now that are not being used as much as they should be? How can you leverage current talent to make a company stronger and better right now? How can you make sure you are aware of those skills if the need ever arises? Knowing the bench strength is a great way to lead the market.

Solve Problems

What else can your company provide? **You are no longer in the product or services business; you are in the problem-solving business.** Start to solve your customers' problems. What does this mean to them as the consumer? How can you be relevant in solving their needs?

1. What is your target client going to need? Think both short- and long-term.
2. What do you not offer that you need to start offering?

How can your solutions help your clients? The person who solves it first will gain huge rewards. Think outside the box. What do your clients really value that you can expand on or focus on more directly?

Cash Call

When the markets closed and government relief packages were not clear, it was a panic for businesses to know how they would ensure the bills and staff got paid in a timely way. You can't ask your team to perform miracles if they are worried about their own financial security.

1. Can you pre-sell or bulk sell your service? This is a great solution for a cash crunch or crisis scenario: cash flow.
2. Is there an incentive that you can offer for prepayment?

Getting your current customers to really invest in your longevity is the best scenario. It does not need a bank loan or long meetings to secure investors. Make yourself indispensable to your clients, and they will happily buy packages and presales with loyalty discounts for something they know they will continue to buy.

Double Down

> *If you find something that works, double down on it.*
>
> *Steve Scott*

Where can you double down? Where in the market have your competitors retreated and left a gap? In many cases, most businesses have stopped marketing altogether. This does not have to be you. You can fill in the gap.

1. Where can you redirect your marketing dollars for the best value?
2. Where can you leap ahead of the industry by continuing to work hard while others are pulling back?

Many businesses stopped marketing altogether. It was odd to scroll social media and not see any ads for anything. People were unsure if they could ship, and contactless door-to-door delivery proliferated in the local communities as companies struggled to deliver on time, with online shopping and deliveries at an all-time high.

Apple Easy

How can you make it easier for your customers to do business with you? What barriers does your current business model create? Evaluate the entire customer journey for out-of-the-box thinking and solutions.

1. Is it easy to do business with us?
2. Is there an innovation we can use to improve our customer experience?
3. Are there any faster, easier, cheaper, or more efficient options worth exploring?

Sometimes we forget to look at our businesses through a new lens because it is just the way it has always been done. This is the perfect time to improve what is wrong with your business model. What prevents this from being your dream business to own? When there are no rules, it is time to build the business you want to own. The one that will create the lifestyle you wish to lead. You get to build it and make it better during a time like this.

Staying Open When the World Closed:

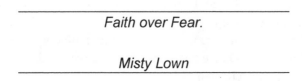

Faith over Fear.

Misty Lown

On March 17th, 2020, the day that our local government mandated that all businesses close, we closed our doors for an indefinite period of time. At that time, our chief medical officer had suggested it might be until the fall. Six long months, not knowing if there would be a business to come back to. We made a decision that we needed to provide some sort of normalcy for our students but also fight to stay in business by providing services online.

I'm sure none of us thought that we would be homeschooling indefinitely at that time, but here we were. I also didn't know that I'd be running a business online that was built in five days with a growth mindset. Our students adapted to our online platform quickly. Shortly, we were receiving feedback from our families that they were over the moon excited about the ability of their children to still have some level of normalcy in their day. They needed to stay connected with an activity that brought them joy in a scary world. We worked hard to create many different outside-the-box experiences for our dancers. For our students, we created family-friendly online challenges, reading clubs, story times with teachers, fashion shows with costumes that never made it to the stage, and more.

It was a time of huge innovation for my team and bonding that we will never forget. It was all-hands-on-deck, and key skill sets that people on my team had but that we had never explored or been aware of before were being featured and regaled by their peers for saving the day! It was a time of teammates stepping up more than ever and rallying around a cause that we all held dear. My staff also reported that without this innovative project, they may have suffered more mental health issues. Being busy was such a blessing in so many ways.

I went to my trusted advisors and my networking group at More Than Just Great Dancing®! to gain critical information about what was happening far and wide around the world. I worked to create that same level of trust and integrity with Dance Safe Alberta and Dance Safe Canada. You will read more about these later in this chapter.

We created a platform that the community at large would be able to interact with and utilize the resources that we had provided for our families. We decided as a company that we would create something for the whole community to access, not just our paying families. This continues to be our mission, to provide as much as we can to all the people we can. Even if our families were unable to afford to continue their lessons, we would continue to bring them along on the journey with us. We provided our community with $34,000 in scholarships between April – and June of 2020. We are so proud of that! Our online platforms included live virtual classes, as well as pre-recorded material, a student lounge that was a safe space for students to communicate, free dance resources, an activity area where crosswords and pictures could be downloaded, free educational resources for all families to access, storytime with our teachers in recorded format for students, and an area with government resources for families.

In less than five days, we moved 125 dance classrooms, music classrooms, and theatre classrooms onto the Google Classroom platform. Our Google classrooms had easy-to-follow instructions and interactions with their teachers. Students were able to take classes and upload practice videos for feedback if they wished. We had tested all of our online content, we had an easy-to-use no-Google-account-necessary format, with live streaming of classes, recorded choreography, videos, combos, warm-ups, and more. New resources were added weekly, as well as weekly live gatherings to keep our APA families together and our community alive.

We continue to share with our families that when we had made the decision a couple of years earlier and committed our savings to grow the business with the addition of new studio space, we had never dreamed that we would be confronted with a collapsing oil economy causing an economic downturn, and a pandemic at the same time. We reminded them that we were strong and humble, that we had been shaken and there was fear. But more so, there was hope that we were creating safety for our families, and we were still a safe space for your child. We reiterated that we were grateful for their ongoing support and patience as we navigated uncharted territory.

We reopened over the summer of 2020. We were in the process of regaining our client base and enjoying seeing faces back in the studio again when an unthinkable second wave and second closure happened. We were closed longer this time – almost four months. During the summer, we improved on our online classroom portals. We invested in a more robust platform that allowed us to have an even better customer experience. We hired a VA (virtual assistant) to help us continue to upload weekly content into the student classrooms. We invested heavily in teacher training that would allow them to effectively teach students both in-person and who were safer at home, attending online. We worked hard to figure out the most engaging way to teach and keep students engaged in the online setting.

When we re-opened, we proudly launched even more than we had during closure. We reopened as a Tech Enabled™ Studio, ready to provide hybrid learning online or in-person no matter your reason. We had invested in large TVs for each room and new sound equipment so that kids learning from home would have better audio and our recordings would have much-improved quality.

We opened with our Safer Studio™ Strategies. This was a document that outlined all the changes to our facility to ensure our students and staff were safe during operational hours. It spoke to our entrance and exit procedures, how to come prepared for class, and the cleaning procedures that were sanitizing everything and how frequently. It spoke to how we understood a closed lobby was a concern, so we had student teachers who were helping get students to and from class safely while earning leadership skills, and ways for parents to view classes from their cars, since the lobby was not available for viewing as it previously had been. We spoke to the concerns that parents had about returning to class during public health restrictions.

For our staff, we had to ensure that their hours were protected and that we had enough staff to cover if anyone had to leave a shift suddenly to protect the workplace. We replicated the studio sound systems by investing again in equipment so teachers teaching from home could still provide excellent classes and recordings of quality. Now teachers could teach from home or studio, and students could learn from home or studio. We were able to work with our staff to cross-train them on monitoring rooms if the regular teaching was off-site. We did equipment checks to ensure that everyone had their equipment optimized and would not have an issue switching at a moment's notice.

The last piece of the puzzle was ensuring the kids would have great learning experiences at home. We initiated personalized prop bags for items that used to be classroom-shared, like wands, scarves, and maracas. Every dancer had a list of things that they would purchase and have with them for either classroom use or learn–from-home use, and it allowed us to continue to give a great class no matter where you were.

At the time of writing, we are partially open with small numbers and physically distanced classrooms. We have learned that our customers are truly concerned about protected investments and short-term commitments. We have a schedule that is heavy with sessional classes that are four-week commitments, and our families are slowly building consumer trust with us again.

The effects of this are long-term and will continue to be felt for years. Savings have been wiped out and loans are owed above and beyond the programs our government provided in the hopes of keeping the economy viable.

We have also turned the business model on its end to create a company that will serve us and fix what is a broken business model. We have five hours a day, six days a week, to make money, and only 10 months out of the year. At the end of every season, we say goodbye to every single customer and hope they come back. Then we spend the summer hustling to ensure we will have enough students enrolled to do it all over again in the fall. On top of that, every summer you risk losing your staff because they have no income to speak of for two months while there is no work.

This is a broken system.

We set out to create a company that would ensure the staff are taken care of and that we do not risk closing every summer that comes along. We now operate 11 months out of the year and run just a few weeks of camps during the 12th month (July). We have created 12-month payment plans for families to have better rates for the activities they take with us all year long. We introduced registration that keeps our students enrolled until they opt-out, rather than re-enrolling everyone each new year. By making these few small adjustments to our business model, we are able to better sustain our bills and payroll. We are a much more stable company with staff that feel important, cared for, and valued for their specialized skill sets.

It took a pandemic to be able to correct the things that made this a hard business to own. But I am proud of what we have accomplished and how we came together to do it. A growth mindset absolutely is what got us through. As I spoke to others in other industries, it was clear that being a lifelong learner and optimist, in general, were key factors in our ability to stay in the game and rise up on the other side. We are poised for unprecedented growth after unprecedented times, and it is exciting to think about what we will be able to accomplish in the recovery years.

Through all of this, I co-founded Dance Safe Alberta and Dance Canada Council alongside two other studio owners. We have amassed a community of owners and teachers with almost 400 people at the time of writing.

The purpose of Dance Safe Alberta is to advocate and educate for the safety of our businesses to the government while they work to create sector guidance. Our short-term goal is to be at the table for re-opening conversations with regulators and to better understand how our industry can be part of the solution province-wide. We seek to educate the government on the differences between dance as education and dance as sport.

Our long-term goal is to create an association that can serve dance and performing arts similarly to how provincial sports organizations serve other sports in our province. Our purpose is to bring structure, consistency, safety, and educational growth to studio owners, operators, educators, and participants.

Dance Safe Canada Council was also born of the pandemic and the need for an industry association nationwide. Our mission is to bring structure, consistency, safety and educational growth to dance and performing arts business owners, operators, organizations, educators, and participants in Canada.

Author's Note

Everything you need to be great is already inside you. Stop waiting for someone to light your fire. You have the match.

Darren Hardy

Now you know my journey of where I came from. It was not always pretty and definitely not the easy way most days. But it is my story, and it has shaped me into an incredibly resilient, mentally tough, and shrewd businessperson with a huge heart. Now let me share where I am going.

I am destined to be a serial entrepreneur. It is the spirit that ignites my fire every day, to create something where there was nothing before. I am forever an artist shaping the world around me and creating a future that is bright and exciting with new ideas and opportunities daily.

I have created several different companies, all while nurturing my first company. I created Classion Designs Corp. with my life partner over four years ago. This company solves the problems that I encountered with importing products from the United States and overseas. As a Canadian company, we encounter terrible issues and exponential costs with importing, from brokerage fees to taxes of up to 45% on textiles and awful currency exchange rates. I decided I was done with the unknown, and my life partner and I have worked hard to solve many of the issues created by the need to import costumes, shoes, and class wear. Along the way, we discovered we could pass the savings on to other studio owners, and before long, a new company was born.

I have also taken my love of teaching into the business world. Forever an educator, I am determined to help other owners not make the same mistakes I did. My mistakes were costly and painful at times, and if I had a mentor like me early on, I would have made many different decisions. I created my consulting business through my desire to help others and, where I can, shorten the distance for learning and results. I am entering the stage of my life where it is more important to give back to others and raise them up than it is to push forward. I am hard-wired to lift people up, in my classroom, in my management team, and in my business community. It is such fulfilling and important work. Our society is in deep need of leadership – heartfelt and thoughtful leadership.

I have found a new stage, now that I am no longer performing as a dancer. I have found great joy in speaking at conferences, creating content to teach others, and writing magazine articles, presentations, and books. I have experienced so much in my years and experiences that I want to ensure all my knowledge is available to anyone who is seeking to learn a better path forward. You can get access to several digital tools for this book here:

https://tarapickford.com/teachingambitionresources

I am determined to leave my family a legacy that provides and could be carried on if they wish. I have also been blessed to be in the position to now own real estate that furthers my legacy and impact. I am able to provide a safe and healthy home to a family in a rental house, and house my studio in a condo building that I own and build equity in. I am proud to say that after almost setting the whole thing on fire only a few short years ago, it is now a source of pride, more than it ever was at the beginning.

I am excited for a world of business post-pandemic. There are so many opportunities for those who can see the blue sky and raise a team of people who can work alongside them to realize the vision I can paint.

I continue to sit on various boards in the dance and local communities. It is important to show my own children how to be a good stewards of the community we live in. To help them grow into contributing members of society. To give my talents and time where possible to better our world. To be available to them and guide their journey into their own.

I say all this because how you show up to some people is how you show up to all people. I walk the walk and talk the talk. It is not easy to lead by example every day, and there are days where it is very difficult to breathe on the high road, but I like to remind myself that's how you know you are on the high road. Giving grace to others and yourself is a daily challenge, and sometimes as Covid has shown, it can be an hourly challenge. The grit the life of an entrepreneur requires is intense. Your feet will always be to the fire with the next idea or innovation. *Grace and grit* are a staple for every single day my feet hit the ground.

Teaching ambition is something I have been doing for almost 30 years. Whether it is a three-year-old learning to be independent, a grade-school student reaching a heartfelt goal, or a high-school student gaining entry to education or a job that they have worked hard for. Maybe it is a team member who wants to reach for more on my leadership team. I am all in **every day** for the people in my life. Forever a teacher at heart, I will never stop looking for opportunities to create tomorrow's leaders in all aspects of my life. We need leaders with heart and vision, compassion and wisdom, now more than ever.

I think my greatest ambition in life is to pass on to others what I know.

Frank Sinatra

Acknowledgement

Special thank you to Big Sky Authors, especially Tammy Plunkett for helping me bring this book into reality. To Misty Lown for being the best mentor who came along at just the right time. Thank you to my parents for those first dance lessons; you never know how the arts will change a life. To Darren for your endless support and patience with my passion.

About the Author

Tara Pickford is a speaker, author, and serial entrepreneur. As the owner and CEO of Ambition Performing Arts, Classion Designs, and Pickford Consulting, Tara spends most of her time raising tomorrow's leaders. Her focus is on both the arts and providing direction and mentorship to business communities. Tara dedicates her life to teaching others how to be more and to reach further. When not mentoring, speaking, advocating, or consulting, Tara can be found teaching a dance class or spending quality time with her family in Airdrie, Alberta.